Meditations from the Oratory of Divine Love

Life
in Christ

Meditations from the Oratory of Divine Love

Life
in Christ

FR. BENEDICT J. GROESCHEL, C.F.R.
GERARD AND YOLANDA CLEFFI

Our Sunday Visitor Publishing Division
Our Sunday Visitor, Inc.
Huntington, Indiana 46750

Contents

Introduction

This book is the third of four volumes outlining prayer meetings for devout Catholics. It contains weekly meditations first composed for prayer groups who wished to meditate and pray together on the truths of the Catholic faith. The first of such groups in history, made up of devout informed laity, goes back to the late fifteenth century, which was a time of great turmoil and scandal in the Church. A number of priests and people, under the inspiration of St. Catherine of Genoa (1447–1510), banded together to study the Bible and Church teachings, joining their study to a life of serious prayer and good works. A laywoman known as Caterinetta Fieschi Adorna, St. Catherine was director of the Pammatone in Genoa, the largest charity hospital in the world. She and her spiritual followers called the first prayer groups Oratories of Divine Love. The Italian word for prayer group is *oratorio*, which in turn is derived from the Latin word for prayer, *oratio*.

The Oratory of Divine Love was revived in America at the beginning of the new millennium as part of an effort by the

Franciscan Friars of the Renewal to encourage Church reform. Although these meditations were written specifically for the Oratory, the simple outline and structure are not restricted to the Oratory or its members. We hope that they will be helpful to all who wish to grow in their faith and in the love of God and neighbor. Any group of devout people can grow and learn using these meditations, whether at weekly meetings or on their own.

Members of the Oratory today, as in the past, bind themselves to leading a devout life, to reverent participation in the liturgy, and to virtuous works of charity and religion. Oratorians still take on good works; for example, helping out at soup kitchens and other works for the needy, visiting the sick and homebound, and regular friendly visits to the elderly. Today, works of religion can include pro-life activities; assisting in a parish, especially in religious education; or being an extraordinary minister of the Eucharistic to the homebound.

These books of Oratory meditations are being published one volume each year over the course of four years to make a complete cycle of Catholic faith and Scripture. When complete, each of the books will correspond to one of the four parts of the *Catechism of the Catholic Church*:

Book I. The Profession of Faith
Book II. The Celebration of the Christian Mystery

Book III. Life in Christ
Book IV. Christian Prayer

Book I, *Praying with the Creed*, examined the truths of the Catholic faith as outlined in the Creed. Book II, *Experiencing the Mystery of Christ,* moved us on to the second phase of our prayer journey: the consideration of the sacraments and liturgy — that is, Christ's work in union with the Holy Spirit to bring the blessings of the heavenly Father into our lives and world. This third book considers the way that Christ expects us to live as His disciples, that is, the pattern of behaviors that he wants us to embrace in order for us to live moral and holy lives. It will be helpful for readers of this book to have on hand a copy of the *Catechism*, with which they will become familiar.

Those who meet only sporadically should try to cover each of the meditations given here, even if on their own. It is advisable to limit meetings to an hour, or perhaps an hour and a half, to avoid tedium. It is important to keep in mind that the overall plan for this series is to follow the *Catechism* with its four major divisions.

The original Oratories selected a reader who served for six months and coordinated the meeting. A group may also suggest someone as a permanent secretary, who corresponds with a central Oratory and tends to simple business matters, such as where meetings will be held, and circulates information about sick or needy members. It is intended that the structure and operations of the Oratory be very simple.

Whether you belong to the Oratory or not, we hope that you will find this book spiritually beneficial. Further, we hope that the serious study of the Scriptures and the Catholic faith will make you a deeper witness to the saving grace of Our Lord Jesus Christ and an active participant in the work of reform of the Church. Reform is just beginning and can be seen particularly in the young people known as the John Paul II generation. There is much to do, as Pope Benedict XVI has indicated: the restoration of a sense of awe and reverence; the renewal of Catholic education, which is often mediocre when not positively destructive; the strengthening of the priesthood with the resurrection of religious life; and the work of loving care for the poor and unfortunate.

Your participation in the weekly Oratory meditations may prove spiritually beneficial to you or to your group. If they do, we would be grateful to hear from you at the Oratory:

> Oratory of Divine Love
> P.O. Box 1465
> Bloomfield, NJ 07003

INTRODUCTION

This volume of meditations and prayers for the members of the Oratory of Divine Love has been prepared by Jerry and Yolanda Cleffi. Every week, they faithfully produce meditations for the Oratory's Web site on the Internet (www.oratorydl.com), from which these are adapted.

I am very grateful to the Cleffis for this work, as well as for their faith and their interest in helping so many people enrich their spiritual lives with these meditations. I am also grateful to John Collins, my editor, who has prepared these meditations for publication and made the adjustments that were necessary to put them into book form.

I hope you will pray for all four of us as we try to keep these meditations before the members of the Oratory and the wider public.

— Fr. Benedict J. Groeschel, C.F.R.

Meditation One

Man: The Image of God

READINGS
Genesis 1:26-31; Colossians 1:15;
Catechism of the Catholic Church § *1700-1715*

I n the first chapter of the book of Genesis, God says:

"Let us make man in our image, after our likeness; and let them have dominion over the fish of the sea, and over the birds of the air, and over the cattle, and over all the earth, and over every creeping thing that creeps upon the earth. So God created man in His own image, in the image of God he created him; male and female he created them. And God blessed them and God said to them, be fruitful and multiply."

— Gen 1:26-28

We've heard these words untold times before; they are famous, familiar. In fact, they are so well known that perhaps we have ceased to comprehend how mysterious they really are.

What can the true significance of these words be? What can it mean to be created in the image of God? We are finite beings; God is infinite. God is eternal; we are marked by death. We are sinful, frail, the repositories of a thousand imperfections; God is utterly perfect, without fault, goodness itself. What, then, can we have that is so much in common with our Creator that we, flesh and blood creatures, are said to share in the divine image — a gift that even the angels seem to be denied?

Countless answers to this question have been imagined since the days of the Book of Genesis, and we can be sure that there will be innumerable more in the future. To the artist, man displays the image of God by creating works of beauty and emotional depth: poems, symphonies, paintings, dances, and dramas that resonate within the human heart. To the scientist, the image of God within us becomes apparent as we unravel the mysteries of the material world, as we compel the vast universe to yield us its secrets. To the saintly, the image of God is revealed when we are compassionate, when we forsake self-interest for love of others. In all of these things, and many more, we catch glimpses of the image of God in man; these glimpses are brilliant flashes of light that reveal us as being different from the rest of creation, as being part of the world yet not entirely possessed by it.

As Christians, we emphatically deny something that many others tell us we cannot deny: that the essence of human life is located in the human body. We are unshakably convinced that we are more than the sum total of our biochemical processes, of our cells and neurons and molecules, of our genetic structure and conditioning. Neither do we believe that our essence can be found in anything related to our brief moment on earth. Rather, the very core of our being, the thing that makes us truly human, is the soul that God breathes into us. It is our certitude that we find our essence in this unimaginable gift of soul, a soul that is spirit as God is spirit, is eternal as God is eternal, is free as God is free. It is the gift of soul that enables us to love as God loves and unites all the disparate parts of our being into a whole person, thus making us the one true image, the only real reflection of the divine power that brought all things into being.

In bestowing this divine image upon us, our heavenly Father has linked us to Him in a way that no other part of creation is. This intimate connection is what makes a life lived without God frustrating, empty, and ultimately tragic, and it is the reason that every human life can accurately be described as a search for God. St. Augustine perceived this clearly and wrote: "Our souls are restless until they rest in you." We spend our lives searching for our heavenly Father as one might search for the missing piece of a puzzle. Without that vital piece, our lives remain incomplete.

MEDITATION ONE

In the book of Leviticus, God tells us, "You shall be holy; for I the Lord your God am holy" (Lev 19:2). Only we who carry the divine image have the capacity for holiness; only we can mirror the One who is holiness itself. So often, however, we are far from holy. Original sin and the many actual sins of our lives cloud our vision and deform our desires. We make our own rules rather than follow the commands of the One whose image we bear. Out of love God grants us free will, and we use it to replace Him with idols of our own creation. We willingly embrace sin, and the image of God within us seems to grow faint.

But even the worst of our sinfulness cannot destroy the love of God or totally obliterate His image within us. In Christ "the image of the invisible God" (Col 1:15) we were created, and in Christ we are redeemed. In our divine Savior's taking on of our human image, in His dying for us on Calvary, and in His rising again, He restores to its original brilliance the divine image within us. He makes it possible for us to reflect God's holiness once again, to be holy as God is holy. We find new life in Christ as he renews the divine image in us and makes real the Psalmist's words: "What is man that thou art mindful of him, and the son of man that thou dost care for him? Yet thou hast made him little less than God, and dost crown him with glory and honor" (Ps 8:4-5).

MAN: THE IMAGE OF GOD

Quotation for Meditation

[T]he whole of man is seen as created in the image of God. This perspective excludes interpretations which locate the *imago Dei* in one or another aspect of human nature (for example, his upright stature or his intellect) or in one of his qualities or functions (for example, his sexual nature or his domination of the earth). Avoiding both monism and dualism, the Bible presents a vision of the human being in which the spiritual is understood to be a dimension together with the physical, social and historical dimensions of man.

Secondly, the creation accounts in Genesis make it clear that man is not created as an isolated individual: "God created mankind in his image, in the image of God he created them, male and female he created them" (Gen 1:27). God placed the first human beings in relation to one another, each with a partner of the other sex. The Bible affirms that man exists in relation with other persons, with God, with the world, and with himself. According to this conception, man is not an isolated individual but a person — an essentially relational being.

— International Theological Commission's
Communion and Stewardship:
Human Persons Created in the Image of God (§ 9-10)

MEDITATION ONE

✎ Quiet Time and Then Discussion ✎

Questions for Meditation

1. In what way does the human person reflect the image and likeness of God?
2. In what ways can we tarnish the image of God within us?
3. In what ways can we enhance the image of God within us?

Prayer

Almighty God, You wonderfully created man in Your own image and did more wonderfully restore him; grant, we beseech You, that as Your Son, Our Lord Jesus Christ, was made in the likeness of men, so we may be made partakers of the divine nature; through the same Son, who lives and reigns with You and the Holy Spirit, one God, world without end. Amen.

Our Vocation to Beatitude

READINGS
Proverbs 16:19; Matthew 5:1-12; 25:14-23;
Catechism of the Catholic Church § *1716-1729*

At the beginning of His active ministry, Jesus gathered the twelve men who would become His apostles. Not long after this he delivered what people throughout the world have come to call the Sermon on the Mount. In this famous discourse Our Lord enunciated the beatitudes, providing a pattern of life for all who would attempt to follow Him, a pattern that leads to holiness and eventually to God. Well known to us all, the beatitudes are found in their most complete form in the Gospel of St. Matthew. They are startling and tell us things that seem to make no sense when viewed through the eyes of the world. The beatitudes remind us that despite what we may think, in the eyes of God:

Blessed are the poor in spirit, for theirs is the kingdom
  of heaven.
Blessed are they who mourn, for they shall be com-
  forted.
Blessed are the meek, for they shall possess the earth.
Blessed are they who hunger and thirst for justice, for
  they shall be satisfied.
Blessed are the merciful, for they shall obtain mercy.
Blessed are the pure of heart, for they shall see God.
Blessed are the peacemakers, for they shall be called
  sons of God.
Blessed are those who are persecuted for righteousness'
  sake, for theirs is the kingdom of heaven.

— Mt 5:3-11

These eight surprising statements set the Christian apart
from the rest of the world; they are daunting, difficult, demand-
ing. In fact, they are not really attainable by human effort alone,
no matter how fervent or persevering we may be. This pattern of
life, set before us by Christ, is attainable only when we depend
on God, when we cooperate with the driving force of the Holy
Spirit. Even so, the beatitudes take a lifetime to follow properly.
But when they are made an integral part of our lives, they transform us, as they have transformed countless others before us. In

a sense, we can say that if we truly live the beatitudes they will make us saints.

From their very first words, the beatitudes challenge us; they force us to stop and think; they make us wonder. "Blessed are the poor in spirit," says Christ, "for theirs is the kingdom of heaven" (Mt 5:3). What does it mean to be poor in spirit, and how can poverty of any kind be such an advantage that it could bring about the kingdom of heaven in one's life?

We are fallen creatures, tainted by sin, and we yearn to possess all that we can. The thought of being poor terrifies us. In our eyes, the poor have failed miserably, and we crave success — success on our own terms. We demand that our will should prevail, even if it is in conflict with the will of God. We proudly imagine that fulfillment and happiness will be ours, if only we can be self-reliant. Thus, we put ourselves in direct opposition to the pattern graciously offered to us by Christ in His Sermon on the Mount. We turn away from holiness; we turn toward sin.

On the other hand, a poor spirit — one that is humble and meek before God — suggests a life lived in harmony with the divine will. Those who are blessed with such a spirit understand the proper order of things. They are able to acknowledge God as creator and themselves as beloved but imperfect creatures. The poor in spirit are able to recognize the primary fact of our lives: that we owe our existence and everything else to our heavenly Father and that we can really possess nothing except the love of God, a possession that gives us abundance beyond comprehension.

Such a "poor" spirit is not easily acquired. We fight against it constantly. To become poor in spirit, we must be willing to die to self, to come to understand that we already have all that we really need in our Father's love. Human will is strong, however, and it is difficult to surrender our multitude of desires. We even have difficulty making small sacrifices during Lent. But we must persevere, for the Holy Spirit will help us if we do.

Our human nature can be compared to a wild stallion. Beautiful and strong, he is a law unto himself and potentially a danger to others. After being tamed, the stallion loses nothing of his beauty or his strength, but acting in harmony (in relationship) with his trainer, he is no longer a threat to anyone. To follow the pattern of life called for by our divine Savior in His Sermon on the Mount, we must allow the Holy Spirit to tame our unruly human natures until our lives become ones of ongoing conversion, until we live more and more in harmony with the divine will, and until we can joyfully proclaim: "Ours is the kingdom of heaven!"

Quotation for Meditation

The Beatitudes speak of something far greater than happiness; that mysterious reality called *blessedness*. But what does this enigmatic word mean? *Webster's* defines it as "enjoying the bliss of heaven." Some people don't find it hard to imagine this type of happiness. They say to me, "Well, you know, I have experienced blessedness. I have at odd moments been truly happy, blessed, even joyful in my poverty before God." Or they may say, "I have experienced God's peace in the midst of mourning the loss of a loved one." I myself have known such moments of blessedness. If you have as well, then you may have had a true taste of the bliss of heaven.

— Fr. Benedict J. Groeschel, C.F.R.,
Heaven in Our Hands, 21

⚜ Quiet Time and Then Discussion ⚜

Questions for Meditation

1. Is it a struggle for you to live the Beatitudes? Try to identify the obstacles you are facing.

2. In what way can your group help each individual better follow the Beatitudes?
3. How can identifying the obstacles and developing a plan to overcome them benefit you? How can it help your group?

Prayer

Lord Jesus Christ, You see all things as they truly are:

In Your eyes, the poor are greatly blessed. Bless us with the grace to be poor as You were poor. Quiet our hunger for possessions and increase in us the yearning for Your friendship.

You gaze upon those who mourn and enfold them in Your love. Bless us with the grace to comfort the sorrowing among us.

You see the meek and shower the good things of the earth upon them. Bless us with the grace to forsake our anger and our pride and to become humble, as You were humble.

You perceive untold misery among us, the fruit of indifference and cruelty. Bless us with the grace to work for justice in our broken world.

You look upon all with infinite mercy. Bless us with the grace to be merciful to others.

You observe the secrets we desperately conceal in the depths of our hearts. Bless us with the grace to be pure of heart, so we may come to know You as You are.

You see God's peace reign in all places but the human soul. Bless us with the grace to be makers of peace at all times.

We see You persecuted every day of our lives. Bless us with the grace to protect the weak and strive for righteousness, so that the kingdom of heaven may at last be ours. Amen.

Meditation Three

Man's Freedom

～©

READINGS
Genesis 2:15-3:7; Sirach 15:11-21; Galatians 5:1;
Catechism of the Catholic Church § *1730-1748*

To be human is to be different. Made in the image and likeness of God, we are a part of creation and yet, somehow, we stand apart from it as well. As bearers of the divine image, we reflect certain of the characteristics of the One who created us. Such reflections are dim, frequently obscured — but they exist, and they distinguish us from the rest of our world. Perhaps our freedom is the most obvious way in which humankind mirrors God. Our heavenly Father is perfectly free. No power can limit His choices; nothing can infringe on His will. For Him, all things are possible, and in His infinite possibility, God graciously shares with His human creation the awesome gift of freedom. Through it, He offers us a way to become a little more like Him.

Limited by a thousand factors outside us and nearly as many within us, our human freedom seems somehow small, frail, and insignificant when compared to the divine freedom, but it is not. It is among the greatest of the heavenly gifts with which we are blessed. It is also the only such gift that we can turn against ourselves, against others, and even against God. Freedom of will — of thought, of action — confer great power on the human soul. Allowing us to choose the good in a very pure way, it enables us to draw close to God, to willingly assent to His will in our lives. It also bestows upon us the ability to sin.

No animal, not even one who has killed a hundred times, has ever murdered, for no animal understands what it does when it destroys another life, and no animal really chooses to draw blood; it simply does what instinct and conditioning demand of it in a given situation.

We, however, are another story; our freedom gives weight and meaning to our actions. We cannot claim that our acts are inevitably imposed upon us by millions of years of evolution or that the events of our past make the actions of our present unavoidable. Every act we perform is one we have chosen; it belongs to us; it is no one else's. In this choosing, we decide between guilt and glory.

To live a human life is to be confronted by choices — many of them agonizing — that are brought into being by God's gift of freedom. One of the many ways in which Holy Scripture can be read is as a succession of choices made by people, choices that bring them closer to the love of God or (all too frequently) farther from it. In the book of Genesis, we encounter the first choice ever to confront humankind. God tells Adam and Eve not to eat of the tree of knowledge of good and evil, that doing so will bring them death. Of course, Adam and Eve were free, as we are free, and they used their freedom to disobey God, to choose the first sin. In this story, our first parents yearned to be as great as the One who had created them. They wanted what was His, not theirs. This yearning, this desperate wanting, led to sin, and sin led to a sad diminishment rather than an enhancement of their lives. By choosing to disobey, Adam and Eve did not forfeit their freedom, yet they found themselves living the lives of slaves — slaves to sin. Their choice separated and alienated them from God, rupturing the one relationship that brought them joy and endowed their freedom with meaning and purpose.

We follow too well in the footsteps of Adam and Eve, using our freedom to choose dishonesty over honesty, self-interest over compassion, idols over God. The tragic choice of Adam and Eve illustrates the entrance of original sin into human life. When we choose our own desires over the will of God, we, too, open the door to sin, inviting it into our lives. In so doing, we obscure the divine image that we carry.

The pull of sin is strong and often seems to become stronger over time. The desire to have our own way sometimes seems irresistible. It is not! God's gift of freedom always leaves many paths open to us, enabling us to turn to the one whose love brought us into being, to choose to submit our will to His. In fact, the gift of freedom permits us to do so at any point, for God never restricts our ability to seek Him no matter how sinful we become. It is the ultimate use of our freedom to choose what is good, to choose the ultimate good — to choose God.

As Holy Scripture presents us with the story of Adam and Eve's misuse of their freedom, so Holy Scripture gives us many examples of those who freely turned toward God when they could easily have turned in different directions. How frightening and confusing must the angel Gabriel's message have been to our Blessed Mother — yet she made the choice that few people would have made, and in so doing, she made possible the salvation of us all. How difficult life must have been in ancient Palestine — yet twelve men cast off whatever security they had ever known to follow an itinerant rabbi who possessed nothing, who could offer them none of the things their world valued. Their choice was absurd — yet, because the apostles made it, the Church was born, and the Gospel has been spread throughout the world.

Such choices must have been wrenchingly difficult to make, yet they were made in freedom, and they still reverberate throughout the world. We, too, must use our awesome gift of freedom to choose as the apostles chose, to choose as Mary chose . . . and so to transform our lives and, perhaps, our world.

Quotation for Meditation

It is . . . only in freedom that man can turn himself towards what is good. The people of our time prize freedom very highly and strive eagerly for it. In this they are right. Yet they often cherish it improperly, as if it gave them leave to do anything they like, even when it is evil. But that which is truly freedom is an exceptional sign of the image of God in man. For God willed that man should be "left in the hand of his own counsel" so that he might of his own accord seek his creator and freely attain his full and blessed perfection by cleaving to him. Man's dignity therefore requires him to act out of conscious and free choice, as moved and drawn from a personal way from within, and not by blind impulses in himself or by mere external constraint. Man gains such dignity when, ridding himself of all slavery to the passions, he presses forward towards his goal by freely choosing what is good.

— *Gaudium et Spes*, #17

❧ Quiet Time and Then Discussion ❧

Questions for Meditation

1. Explain what true freedom is.
2. How can we utilize our freedom to promote personal sanctity?
3. In what ways have we used our freedom to turn away from God?

Prayer

~∾

Father, Son, Holy Spirit,

You are the source of all good things, the profligate giver of gifts.

You bestow life upon us; You offer us eternity; You bless us with the capacity to love.

You even give us freedom, showering us with an infinity of choices.

Give us, we pray, yet one more gift — the gift to use our freedom well.

Enable us to make the right choices, the holy choices, the choices that accord with Your will. Let us never use Your awesome gift of freedom, to turn our backs on You or on each other. Amen.

Meditation Four

The Morality of Human Acts

READINGS
Matthew 6:2-4; Luke 18:9-14;
Catechism of the Catholic Church § 1749-1761

A man has $500,000. His wife is overjoyed; she wants him to use it to redo their home, to transform their modest house into a showplace. His children beg him to spend the money on a family trip to Europe, to buy them expensive new cars and to send them to the best colleges. His friends give him stock tips, assuring him that all he needs to do is wait a few months and he will be a millionaire. He ignores them all, declaring that he has accumulated the money for one purpose: to help others. He donates it all to a charity that cares for children in Third-World countries. Starving babies are fed and lives are saved with this money. The man's family and friends suspect they are in the presence of a saint. Only the man himself knows that the $500,000 was money he embezzled from his employer over many years. He takes this secret to his grave.

The leader of a tiny, faraway country confronts a serious problem. A small ethnic group within his nation demands secession. They have rebuffed all his desperate overtures for peace and have taken up arms. Conflict and death on a grand scale seem inevitable. The leader knows his duty and resolves to choose the higher good. He sends his army to destroy the rebels in a surprise attack. Many are killed, but many more lives are thus saved; peace and tranquility return. He is a hero.

A woman despises her teenaged daughter. The girl, an only child, is doted on by the woman's husband. Tired of sharing the attention she believes she alone deserves, the woman wants to be rid of the girl — a child she never wanted in the first place. She saves her money, denying herself many things. She uses the money to send her daughter to a school far away, a school the girl has dreamed of attending but assumed she would never see. The girl is ecstatic; the father is saddened; the woman is pleased that she has finally found a way to create the life that she always wanted.

Are these acts morally good or bad? Each of them clearly resulted in good. Just as clearly, none of them was totally good; each seemed tainted in some way. Like so much of life, these three little stories seem ambiguous and uncertain. Perhaps we see in them our own problems in distinguishing right from wrong, in choosing among competing goods. Yet we must choose, for we are human and choice confronts us constantly.

St. Thomas Aquinas, one of the great philosophers of morality, tells us there is a way to do this choosing and offers us three criteria upon which we may base our moral decisions: the objective act, the subjective motive, and the circumstances that surround the situation. For Aquinas and for the Church in general, all three of these factors must be good if an act is to be considered morally good. If even one is not, the act becomes tainted — it becomes morally bad.

In the case of the generous embezzler, the objective act, donating money to charity, is good — laudable, in fact. The subjective motive, to help starving children, is also something we have little difficulty in identifying as good; in fact, it reminds us of Mother Teresa. But then we come to the circumstances: the money that achieved this good was acquired through theft. The good that was accomplished cannot be questioned, but the circumstances poison the act. The generous embezzler cannot claim that his act was good, despite the results. He has sinned greatly.

The beleaguered leader was in a difficult situation. His subjective motive was to preserve the stability of his small nation and to avoid greater bloodshed. This is obviously good. The circumstances, which include his position of responsibility and the fact that he was confronted by a rebellion, made action of some kind not only morally good but necessary. Sending troops to massacre the insurgents, however, can never be justified. Murder can never be good even if we think it is done in the service of a greater good. The objective nature of the act is bad. He has committed a brutal crime.

The woman has made her daughter happy by sending the girl to the school of her dreams, thus opening new and wonderful possibilities for the girl. The objective act is, therefore, above reproach. The circumstances that surround the act, the mother's self-sacrifice, cannot be bad. To deny oneself in order to enable another to accomplish something greatly yearned for is a wonderful act. But the subjective aspect of this act — the desire to rid herself of her daughter's presence — is bad. This act is poisoned, as well.

"Human actions are moral actions," St. Thomas Aquinas tells us. Everything we do can be analyzed in terms of good or evil, and evil has a way of worming itself into acts undertaken with the best of intentions, acts that would otherwise shimmer with mercy and charity. If we claim to follow Christ, we must not allow the things that we do to become tainted by evil. We must concentrate our entire being on choosing only objectively good acts. We must make sure our intent is unstained, and all the surrounding circumstances are holy. This is not easy, for life is fraught with ambiguity. In our fallen world, evil often masquerades as good; often, we think that the greater good justifies a little wrongdoing, that nothing can be pure, and we're just obligated to do the best we can. But things can be pure; our acts can be morally good if we work to make them that way, if we accept God's graces into our lives, into our choosing.

We are human beings and — like it or not — we are free. Choices disclose themselves at every turn, presenting themselves like gifts dropped in our path. A thousand possibilities are ours. We are, indeed, profoundly blessed, but the blessing of freedom does not come to us alone. It comes with its twin: the blessing of responsibility.

Quotation for Meditation

Morality is found in every truly human act. Every deliberate, controlled act of man will take him toward happiness or away from it. The dignity and the power of each man's freedom and control over his own human actions is clear. When a man's controlled command of his own actions is directed by right reason to his last end, then that man is capable of reaching out beyond the space-time limits of the whole universe to the age-less, limitless horizons of the vision of God. When his deliberate, controlled actions are directed against the dictates of right reason to some other goal than perfect happiness then that man is descending into the smallest region of the confining and restraining limits of his own meager self. Good is an expanding force, capable of opening up the soul of man to the limitless vistas of the Divine Being. Evil and sin are constraining and limiting forces, capable of imprisoning man in the narrow confines of his smallest self.

— Walter Farrell, O.P., S.T.M.,
and Martin J. Healy, S.T.D.,
My Way of Life, 185-186

⊰◈ Quiet Time and Then Discussion ◈⊱

Questions for Meditation

1. What have been my standards for determining morally good actions? How do they compare with the ones developed by St. Thomas Aquinas?

2. What are the areas of my life where my choices seem morally questionable?

3. Feelings and emotions are involved in the determination of a morally good or bad act. How can I best control my emotions to make sure they contribute to moral goodness?

Prayer

There are too many choices, Father; and there are too many voices telling me what to do. I want to follow Your will, to do good at all times, but so often I am confused, unable to make a decision, terrified I will make the wrong one and offend You. Send me the inspiration of Your Holy Spirit to guide me in my choosing. Help me to choose only the good. Then I shall be a true child of Yours, and I shall praise You forever. Amen.

Meditation Five

The Morality of the Passions

∿

READINGS
Mark 7:14-23; Luke 23:13-35; Romans 7:13-20;
Catechism of the Catholic Church § 1762-1775

We live in a culture that exalts emotions, that worships the passions. A well-known actress loses her heart to her leading man. Fiercely proud of their new relationship, the two gaze longingly into each other's eyes during a television interview. They speak endlessly of the love that hurled them into each other's arms, a love too powerful to be resisted. Indulgently, the world smiles its approval and eagerly awaits the pictures of their wedding — the third for her, the second for him. Perhaps in a footnote we will be reminded of their most recent spouses, the ones they abruptly deserted in order to be with each other. We may even hear something of the small children they apparently forgot about when passion overcame them, but none of that matters, for our culture will not judge. In fact, many of us will envy them; we almost wish that such powerful emotions would come flooding into our own lives, lifting us out of the banality of daily existence and offering us the happiness that is supposed to be the fruit of such passion.

"I think, therefore I am," the philosopher René Descartes famously wrote, fundamentally changing the way Western man understood himself. "I feel, therefore I am!" screams contemporary culture, striving mightily to change us back again. Today, our emotions, our passions, are proclaimed to be the one true standard by which an authentic life can be lived. We learn that we have only to be honest about our feelings and to act on them. If we do this, then all the rest will fall neatly into place.

As Christians, we simply cannot accept this, for we know that God created us to be more than a mass of feelings, appetites, and yearnings; we understand our souls to be far deeper than that. We stand alone in our world, as creatures endowed with reason, with will, with the inner strength to control our passions — at least at times — and use them for the good of others. We are God's final and most beloved creation and His partners in our own redemption. To permit our emotions to reign over us is to deny the divine image within us; it is to become less than we were meant to be.

Yet the Christian attitude toward the passions is not at all negative. The Church does not try to reject them or tell us to suppress them in any way. The Church honors our emotions, knowing them to be among God's many gifts to us, acknowledging them to have as much potential to bring us to holiness as they do to bring us to ruin. Our ability to experience love, sadness, elation, or even anger is part of what it means to be human. Those few who are untouched by such feelings seem incomplete, pitiable. We should rejoice in our human capacity to feel deeply, to love fully. Powerful passion has often spurred people on to works of great charity, to acts of selfless love. People who were passionately committed to doing God's work on earth have accomplished untold good. It is the dark side of the emotions that the Church warns us of — the anger that becomes destructive rage, the sadness that leads to incapacitating depression, the love that turns into possessiveness, that grasps and devours.

The *Catechism* tells us that love, "the most fundamental passion," is "aroused by the attraction of the good" (*CCC* 1765). Here we find the key to making passion part of our journey to God rather than a distraction from it. If all love — all passion — is caused by an attraction to what we understand to be good, then we can turn our passions toward what is truly good — the will of God. If we assent to God's will with our own human will and with our reason, we have achieved much, but we still remain divided. With the help of the Holy Spirit we are able to turn even our passion to the will of God, to join our emotions to our will and reason, so that when we say "Thy will be done," we assert these words with our whole being. In this way we turn from a world that worships the passions and toward the God who sanctifies them.

Quotation for Meditation

All the passions of man, from love to anger, are powers given to man to enable him to seek what is good and to avoid what is evil. Under the control of reason and will their action can be morally good or bad. The man of many desires can forget God in the pursuit of pleasure. This is what the drunkard or the libertine does. The fearful man can desert God in his desire to avoid all difficulty or pain. The passions must be brought under the control of right reason and will. Their powers must be directed to what is morally good. The passions are like the power in an automobile. As long as the driver is in command of the automobile, the driving power of the car will take him safely where he wishes to go. But if he loses control of the car, both the driver and the car come to grief. When properly directed by right reason the passions move man to accomplishment. They help man to dominate the world for his own happiness and God's glory. When a man loses control and allows himself to be ruled by his passions they lead him to destruction — to the ruin of his human personality.

— Walter Farrell, O.P., S.T.M.,
and Martin J. Healy, S.T.D.,
My Way of Life, 211-212

✎ Quiet Time and Then Discussion ✎

Questions for Meditation

1. What passions control you?
2. Should we feel guilty about our passions?
3. Discuss what you can do to direct or redirect your passions.

Prayer

Eternal Father, I am far too human. My emotions control me; passion sweeps over me like a wave, dissolving my will, carrying me to places I should never visit — places I know too well. Father, help me to order the unruly feelings and confusing emotions that turn my life into such disarray. Give me the grace to resist the forces that pull me in a thousand directions at once. You create peace in the high heavens; create, I beg of You, peace in my heart, as well. Then I will be able to turn to You with my whole being in joy and thanksgiving, eager to do Your will. Amen.

Meditation Six

Moral Conscience

READINGS

Psalm 73:23-25, 119:105-108; Romans 2:12-16; 1 Timothy 1:18-20;
Catechism of the Catholic Church § 1776-1802

Our world is a world of ambiguity. What is condemned as
sin by some is considered simple choice by others. Acts
that once were universally considered morally wrong are now
commonplace — barely noticed. We are subject to relentless
seductions from the culture around us and are told that notions
such as good and evil are plainly out of date. We are preyed
upon by drives from within as well as endless forces from without and are regularly propelled in one direction after another;
desperately searching after things we know we shouldn't want
but feel we cannot live without. We are left shamefaced, full of
regrets. So often we feel that we are failures, that we are hopeless, that we do not know how to live or what to do.

But why should this be? The universe God has placed us in is orderly. Law pervades all things. Stars, solar systems, and galaxies burst into existence following precise laws that astrophysicists have studied. The laws of mathematics are unalterable; using them, we will one day be able to describe the workings of the cosmos. All things from the vast universe itself to the most minute subatomic particle follow our heavenly Father's divine plan at every instant — all things but us, that is.

We sense the divine law as we observe the world around us, in the changing of the seasons, in the cycles of growth and decay, in our relationships with others. We are instinctively aware that some things are wrong to do, that other things are necessary to do. God's orderliness dawns upon our consciousness over and over again reminding us that we, alone of creation, rebel. Our imperfect lives continue to reveal what we already know: that we are fallen creatures all but incapable of helping ourselves. Yet we are still made in the divine image; we are still beloved of God, and our heavenly Father offers us endless ways to heal our sinful natures, including the gift of conscience. Conscience is that "still, small voice within us" that allows man to discover "a law which he has not laid upon himself but which he must obey. Its voice, ever calling him to love and to do what is good and avoid evil, sounds in his heart at the right moment" (*CCC* 1776).

If we turn to conscience fearlessly and truthfully, if we discard personal preference and exchange emotion for reason, if we strive to examine starkly, honestly, and prayerfully the choices with which we are confronted, we will discover that we are alone with God, with truth, with the divine order. We will begin to form our conscience — a process that takes a lifetime — and to conform it to the divine will. We form it by observing the Commandments, the teachings of the Church, by practicing the good (which is not always identical with what we consider to be good for ourselves), by making amends for our failures and striving to learn from them. We will frequently fail, and often our conscience will remain deformed for long periods of time, telling us to do as we please, that God doesn't really mind the occasional sin. But if we persevere, as the days pass and the years vanish, our conscience will slowly grow and gradually mature. Slowly, we will come to perceive the will of God in our lives. We will see ambiguity diminish as we are able to distinguish more and more clearly between good and evil, as we begin to make out our own unique place in God's plan. When our conscience is finally well formed, we will at last comprehend what is truly good, and eventually we may even surrender our rebelliousness and enter into the beauty and serenity of God's orderliness.

Quotation for Meditation

The matter of following one's conscience is crucial. What responsibility do we have to follow what our conscience dictates? Everything depends on the degree of sincere certitude we have in facing a moral decision. We are obliged always to act on the dictates of a conscience that is certain. It must be obeyed even though objectively it may be false, because conscience is the nearest available norm we have for knowing what is right and wrong, and the criterion by which God will judge the human soul. On the other hand, we may never act with a doubtful conscience. So that unless the mind clearly says that a prospective action is permissible, we may not do it. Otherwise we should be saying equivalently, "This may be good or bad, offensive or pleasing to God. But I do not care, and will do it anyway."

— John A. Hardon, S.J.,
The Catholic Catechism, 292

◈ Quiet Time and Then Discussion ◈

Questions for Meditation

1. How does man's fallen nature affect his conscience?
2. What can one do to better form the conscience?
3. What role does emotion play in regard to conscience?

Prayer

Father, You endow man with conscience, the still small voice within us that calls us back to You over and over again when we have strayed and when we are tempted. Help me to form my conscience daily, to search in all my doings for Your ways rather than the ways of the world. Let me never forget that it is better to have the entire world against me than to incur Your divine displeasure for an instant. Give me the gift of a strong and insistent conscience, Father, for with such a conscience as my guide I shall be able to come closer and closer to You.

The Virtues

READINGS
Psalm 1, Proverbs 21:21; 2 Peter 1:3-11;
Catechism of the Catholic Church § 1803-1845

Virtue is a strange word, one we rarely hear. In these early years of the twenty-first century, we might even say that this word has been emptied of whatever significance it once held. If we think of virtuous people at all, our minds turn to the past, perhaps to a time before our grandparents were children. This word conjures up for us thoughts of a simpler world, of people who actually thought they could perceive the difference between right and wrong, of a time when idealism was still possible. That world is gone, and we must work hard even to recall it.

We like to think that we understand ourselves too well, that we are too wise to believe in virtue. Our science delves deeply into the human psyche, laying bare all the tangled complexities and warring forces once hidden there. From psychologists we learn that all our actions are ultimately selfish ones, that we have no souls and are but products of years of conditioning; biologists tell us that our genes predetermine our lives. Thus, the world proclaims a narrow vision of what it means to be a person. It sees us as tiny cogs in a huge machine, one that lumbers inexorably forward, carrying us along with it. In such an understanding of humanity, God is irrelevant, free will an illusion, and virtue a sad joke.

But we have a secret. No matter how powerfully the world's ideas shape our thoughts, no matter how regularly we declare our acceptance of them, something aches within us, and a voice from deep inside proclaims a different vision, one that sees our lives as having meaning and our world as being coherent. No matter what we are told, we believe that we choose our acts. We also see them as either good or bad — and the bad ones haunt us, despite our determined efforts to forget them.

We sense that such an understanding of humanity is more truthful than the one our world proclaims — at least we do during those times when the din of the world becomes muted for a moment or two — and we begin to suspect that virtue might not be a joke after all, that it might even be something to invite into our lives.

At such moments, the Church is there, and her arms, as always, are open. Seemingly the sole champion of virtue in our times, she assures us that virtue is possible for us all, that it is simply "an habitual and firm disposition to do the good" (*CCC* 1803). She urges us to listen to the "still small voice" within us, the voice of conscience that the world can neither hear nor silence, the voice that helps us distinguish good from evil. Virtue, the *Catechism* tells us, "allows the person not only to perform good acts, but to give the best of himself. The virtuous person tends toward the good with all his sensory and spiritual powers; he pursues the good and chooses it in concrete actions" (*CCC* 1803). Here the Church tells us that we have "powers," and urges us to "listen," to "give," to "act," to "choose," to "pursue" to "perform." In so doing, she tells us that the world is wrong; we are not hopelessly in thrall to forces beyond our control, and we decide how our lives are lived. She proclaims us to be capable of choosing virtue and reminds us of the many great saints of the past who displayed virtue on a heroic scale. She shows us how to learn from their lives, how to imitate their holiness — how to become saints of the present.

As our eager and loving teacher, the Church shows us what we have been too blind to see, that virtue can abound, that it can enrich every human life. She gives names to the virtues, enabling us to distinguish one from another. Through the Church we learn of the cardinal virtues, those that play a preeminent role in every life. We learn of prudence, which enables us to discern the true good and the right means of achieving it; we are instructed in justice, which enables us to give what is due to others and to God; we are taught to build fortitude, which enables us to remain firm and constant in our pursuit of the good; and we are urged to practice temperance, which helps us control our many appetites and desires. The Church admonishes us that the cardinal virtues are not easily achieved, that we must work for them tirelessly, but we also learn that the Church will be with us when we fail, that she will lift us up again and again, even when lives of virtue have come to seem impossible.

The Church encourages us by teaching us of the theological virtues. These are gifts beyond our wanting, things we cannot achieve on our own. Bestowed by the Holy Spirit, they enable us to show forth more brightly the image of God within us. Faith is the first of these, enabling us to believe in and trust our heavenly Father and to profess this conviction vibrantly in our lives. Amidst the many difficulties of life, we depend on the virtue of hope, which enables us to fix our eyes and hearts on the God who will never abandon or disappoint us. The third theological virtue is charity, which reflects a life of love for God and neighbor. It has often been said that the greatest of the theological virtues is charity (or love). Without the divine love poured into our hearts, without our making this love real in our encounters with others, we are nothing and our witness to the faith that we uphold is empty.

In the eyes of the world, we are conglomerations of cells and molecules and atoms, a series of biochemical processes that will eventually slow down until one day they burn out. Our brief journey from conception to death will leave no mark, no ripple behind us. Our struggles are meaningless; our loves are predetermined; our lives are a brief prison. In such a world virtue cannot exist, and the effort to attain it is a blatant refusal to face reality. The life that we are offered by the world is untouched by sin or guilt, unmarked by nobility, incapable of holiness; it is a life of occasional pleasure and ultimate bleakness.

On the other hand, the Church claims to see things the world cannot. She sees us as persons made in the image and likeness of God. In her eyes, all that we do is marked by meaning, and she warns us that our acts will reverberate for eternity. The Church declares virtue to be a word brimming with abundant meaning, a concept that can never become outmoded. She tells us that we are not only capable of virtue but that our humanity demands it. The path the Church offers us can be a difficult one, but if we allow the virtues to suffuse our days on earth, we will never know bleakness and we will come to know joy, for our lives will be spent on the path that God Himself has made for us, the one that leads us home to Him.

Quotation for Meditation

Virtue . . . is more than a series of good deeds. It exists in a person's depths. Presumably, there must be some neurological component because we are made up of body, soul, and spirit. However, I think there is something beyond the physical, not perceptible to scientific comprehension — an aspect of virtue that rises from the depth of the soul. Psychology, understood as a science or as philosophy, cannot deal directly with this mysterious aspect of virtue, which in turn is part of a greater mysterious reality that we call the *human being*.

— Fr. Benedict J. Groeschel, C.F.R.,
The Virtue Driven Life, 24

❧ Quiet Time and Then Discussion ❧

Questions for Meditation

1. What is the importance of virtue in the Christian life?
2. How can we work towards the cardinal virtues?
3. How do the lives of the saints help us to better understand virtue?

Prayer

Almighty Father, in Jesus You give us a model of perfection. In His life on earth we see the path to You in heaven. We try to follow Him, but the road is difficult, and — sinful and selfish — we depart from the path again and again. We would be lost if not for the endless gifts You offer us — the possibility of virtue to transform our lives and conform them to Your holy will. Give us the grace, we pray, to embrace Your gifts of faith, hope, and charity and to strive to make real in our lives the virtues of prudence, justice, fortitude, and temperance. Grant that we may lead lives of virtue, loving Father; lives lived on the path of Jesus, the path of happiness, the path to You. Amen.

Meditation Eight

Sin

READINGS

Genesis 3:1-13, Psalms 42:1-3, Psalm 51; Romans 5:12-21; 1 John 5-10;
Catechism of the Catholic Church § 1846-1876

If we say we have no sin, we deceive ourselves, and the truth is not in us. If we confess our sins, he is faithful and just and will forgive our sins and cleanse us from all unrighteousness (1 Jn 1:8-9). In these powerful words from St. John's first letter, we confront two fundamental truths. The first is a truth about us — something we'd prefer to avoid. We are sinful, this passage tells us, in words that couldn't be more direct, that allow no exceptions and offer no loopholes. In these words we must face the fact that sin is an ever-present part of our lives and that it is a dangerous self-deception to believe we are exempt from this terrible reality. In this one sentence, St. John forces us to do what humankind hates to do: to see ourselves as we are, rather than as we pretend to be. This sentence judges us and finds us to be wanting. It reveals the agonizing truth about us: that we are usually incapable of reforming, that we are frequently uninterested in reforming, that we often delight in our sin.

If St. John had put his pen down at the end of that sentence, we would think we were without hope. But, inspired by the Holy Spirit, he wrote on, boldly stating the second of his two great truths, this one about God. He tells us that God is willing — even eager — to forgive. With this knowledge we are made free, free of thinking that we must depend on our own strength to find God, free of thinking that we must become perfect to deserve the love of God. Through these few words, we learn that we have only to turn to our heavenly Father in trust, sincerity, and humility. In that turning, we will find forgiveness and newness of life. St. John's second sentence teaches us that — despite our endless sinfulness — we are offered abundant hope, endless joy, and infinite possibility.

These two short lines give us a great deal to ponder as we contemplate our relationship with our heavenly Father. They contain wonderful words of salvation and astonishing assurances of God's love, but they also make a demand that may be easy to overlook. Although he urges us to rejoice in God's eternal desire to forgive us, St. John also reminds us that we must be God's willing partners in our own salvation, that we must first confess our sins, admit our wrongdoings. In these two biblical sentences we learn that it is up to us to turn to the Father, that we cannot expect to be mere driftwood lifted by the tide of God's love. These words can never be paraphrased as "We don't have to worry because our God doesn't really care what we do. He will always forgive us." Our God really does care what we do; our God insists that we struggle against sin; our God expects us to cooperate with the graces He so abundantly offers us.

We are endowed with a thousand gifts that are denied the rest of creation, and with these gifts comes profound responsibility, including the duty to lead lives of virtue. We deny the image of God within us if we constantly — almost willingly — succumb to sin and simply count on the divine love for endless and effortless forgiveness. God's mercy is infinite, but it does not eclipse His justice. The assurance of divine forgiveness, therefore, in no way excuses us from striving to do the good at all times. Human beings have fallen natures that have been dramatically weakened by the effects of original sin. We weaken ourselves still more with our many actual sins. No matter how we immerse ourselves in sin, however, the image of God still burns within us. We are still able to turn, to respond to our heavenly Father's graces. At first our turning may be so slight as to be imperceptible to others, but it will never be imperceptible to God, who will graciously meet us, forgive us, and renew us. As time goes on, we will become able to accept God's forgiveness more and more deeply into our lives and we will be able to turn more quickly, more eagerly, and more completely. Psalm 42 begins with this beautiful line, "As the hart longs for flowing streams, so longs my soul for thee, O God." How wonderful this line is; how clearly we see in it our own yearning. In the intense heat of arid Palestine a deer yearns for cool, refreshing streams of water. We, too, live in a world made arid by sin, and we desperately yearn for God's life-giving graces to refresh and restore us as no cool water ever could.

The struggle against sin is the human struggle. Each of us is engaged in it, and we know that it will not end until our earthly lives end. This is a fight that often exhausts and frustrates. It is one that we frequently feel that we have lost and that leaves us feeling unable to go on. At times, it seems too difficult to do anything but surrender to the many forms of sin that entice us endlessly. But we must never give up, for the struggle against sin is really the struggle for God. It is the battle to overcome our fallen nature, to be what we should have been all along, and it results in either grandeur or desolation. There is no need to fail in this battle, for our heavenly Father is always waiting for us to turn to Him. We remember the words of St. John; we acknowledge our faults, failings, flaws, and misdeeds; we allow the graces of the Sacrament of Reconciliation to wash us clean again, to enable us to begin again. We turn to Christ in the Eucharist, the inexhaustible source of new life and new strength. Each time we do this, our relationship with God is made a little stronger; each time we do this, we return to the struggle bearing the divine image just a little more clearly.

Quotation for Meditation

My God, I dare not offend any earthly superior; I am afraid — for I know I shall get into trouble — yet I dare offend Thee. I know, O Lord, that, according to the greatness of the person offended against, the greater is the offence. Yet I do not fear to offend Thee, whom to offend is to offend the infinite God. O my dear Lord, how should I myself feel, what should I say of myself, if I were to strike some revered superior on earth? if I were violently to deal a blow upon some one as revered as a father or a priest; if I were to strike them on the face? I cannot bear even to think of such a thing — yet what is this compared with lifting up my hand against Thee? And what is sin but this? To sin is to insult Thee in the grossest of all conceivable ways. This then, O my soul!, is what the sinfulness of sin consists in. It is lifting up my hand against my Infinite Benefactor, against my Almighty Creator, Preserver and Judge — against

Him in whom all majesty and glory and beauty and reverence and sanctity center; against the one and only God.

— Ven. John Henry Newman,
Prayers, Verses and Devotions, 366-367

Quiet Time and Then Discussion

Questions for Meditation

1. What are the sins that most afflict my life?
2. What is the first step we must take in ridding ourselves of sin?
3. Discuss how examining our consciences can help us in confronting our sins.

Prayer

O Lord, may I know myself; may I know You! May I know my own selfishness, ignorance and weakness, and know, too, that You are ready to lift me up and sustain me as I climb toward the spiritual heights You call me to attain. May I distrust myself and trust in You!

Enlighten my mind, that I may see all my sins clearly; soften my heart that I may be truly sorry for them; give me the grace and courage to confess them sincerely and thus obtain Your pardon, through Jesus Christ our Lord and Savior. Amen.

— *The Vatican II Sunday Missal, 1093*

Meditation Nine

The Person and Community

READINGS
Acts 2:42-47; 1 Corinthians 12:12-30; Ephesians 2:19-22;
Catechism of the Catholic Church § 1877-1896

Before the universe existed, there was community. Before the stars and planets exploded into being, relationship was already ancient. Before life appeared on earth, love bound one to another. This community, this relationship, this love is that of the Holy Trinity. Thus, it lies at the very heart of all being. Perfect unity within perfect trinity is the nature of God. In the absolute harmony of Father, Son, and Holy Spirit, we glimpse relationship at its purest, bonds of love so perfect that no dissonance can ever trouble the divine serenity. Here is the ultimate model for all relationships, the daunting example that we imperfect humans must strive to follow if we are to reflect the image of God.

Living in relationship with others, as God lives in relationship, enables us to grow in holiness, to fulfill the potential that our heavenly Father has implanted within us. This concept permeates sacred Scripture. "It is not good that the man should be alone" (Gen 2:18), God says almost immediately after Adam is created, implying that man without relationship is incomplete. Thus, Eve is brought into being, and the first human relationship is born. Together, our first parents are able to know happiness, wholeness, and joy in ways that no solitary being ever could, and they discover a great gift: their relationship enables them to become partners with God in the very act of creation.

Sacred Scripture reveals something of profound importance about our human nature in the story of Adam and Eve. It shows that we cannot truly be the persons God created us to be in isolation — that the need for relationship, the urge to community, is part of the nature of man. As such, it must be one of the many gifts God has given us to lead us to Him.

From the time of our first parents, human relationships have been continually expanding and developing. Families came into being and slowly gave rise to tribes; tribes came together to form larger groups that eventually became nations. Most human lives are lived enmeshed in a multiplicity of relationships and numerous interlocking communities. Yet, as we look around us, we are saddened to see that few of these communities seem able to reflect the divine relationship that should be their ultimate model. The bonds of relationship seem to grow fragile in our time. Marriages come and go; the lure of higher income makes us uproot ourselves and move thousands of miles from family and friends; innumerable small children hardly know their fathers; our cities are filled with people who know no one and are known by no one, whose lives and deaths go unnoticed. The list goes on and on.

"All real living is meeting,"[1] wrote Martin Buber, a Jewish religious thinker who was steeped in biblical wisdom. These words may sound puzzling at first. Perhaps we can paraphrase them as *we cannot live fully unless we meet others fully.* To be human, to show forth the divine image, we must be able to perceive that same image in others. Too often we meet a cab driver, a bank teller, or a waitress; too rarely do we meet the *man* who is the cab driver, the *woman* who is the bank teller, the nervous teenaged *girl* who just started her first job as a waitress. Too often our meetings with such people, and many others, differ little from our encounters with inanimate objects. This is an insult to the divine image that they bear; it is an insult to God, who created us in His image. It is a rejection of relationship, a denial of community. It is not a real meeting, and it is certainly not the way Christ met others.

Over 2,000 years ago, Christ encountered tax collectors, prostitutes, brutal Roman soldiers, and zealots with bloodstained hands. He met them as they really were: frail, confused people, desperate for the love of God. He willingly forgave them their sins and offered them a relationship that brought them new and unending life. In the Church, we are able to meet that same Christ in the Eucharist. He still offers forgiveness and life-giving relationship. As we receive the Risen Christ, we are powerfully united in community with the entire Church, with uncountable people who bear the divine image. In the Eucharist we are made one body, one community. We must not only accept the grace Christ offers us in the Eucharist; we must use it to transform our lives until our every encounter with other people is a real and holy meeting. We must use it to transform our world until human societies at last begin to reflect a glimmer of the overwhelming unity and perfect community of the Holy Trinity.

Quotation for Meditation

There are souls who seek God in Christ Jesus, who accept the humanity of Christ, but who stop there. That is not enough; we should accept the Incarnation with all the consequences it imposes; we should not let the gift of ourselves stop at Christ's own humanity, but should extend it to His mystical body. That is why — never forget this, for I touch here on one of the most important points of the super-natural life — to abandon the least one of our brethren is to abandon Christ

Himself; to bring relief to one of these is to bring relief to Christ in person. When someone hits a part of your body — hits your eye or your arm — it is you yourself on whom the blow lands. In the same way, to strike a blow at our neighbor, whosoever it may be, is to strike a blow at one of the members of the body of Christ; it is to lay hands on Christ Himself.

And that is why Our Lord tells us that whatever we do, of good or of bad, to the least of His brethren; it is to Him that we do it.

Our Lord is Truth itself; what He teaches us cannot be other than based on a super-natural reality. Well, in this, the super-natural reality that faith makes us discover is that Christ, by becoming incarnate, united Himself mystically to the whole of humanity. Not to accept and not to love all those who belong, or can belong, to Christ through grace is not to accept and not to love Christ Himself.

— Blessed Columba Marmion,
Christ, the Life of the Soul, 453

Quiet Time and Then Discussion

Questions for Meditation

1. What is the ultimate model for community?
2. In my encounters with others, do I meet them as people made in the image and likeness of God, or do I meet them as something less?
3. How can isolation from others prevent me from becoming the person God wants me to be?

Prayer

O blessed Lord, who has commanded us to love one another, grant us grace that having received Thine undeserved bounty, we may love everyone in Thee and for Thee. We implore thy clemency for all; but especially for the friends whom Thy love has given to us. Love Thou them, O Thou fountain of love, and make them to love Thee with all their heart, that they may will and speak, and do those things only which are pleasing to Thee.

— St. Anselm, as cited in
The Oxford Book of Prayer, 372

Meditation Ten

Participation in Social Life
The Question of Authority

READINGS
Mark 1:21-28; Romans 13:1-2; 1 Timothy 2:1-2;
Catechism of the Catholic Church *§ 1897-1927*

As Americans, we know we're not supposed to be too fond of authority; in fact, we're supposed to be distrustful of it. We like to think we're a little better than people in countries who give *carte blanche* to their leaders, bestowing nearly total power upon a select few. Some authority is necessary, of course, but we say it must be severely limited. The frailties of human nature are only too obvious, as are the temptations of authority. A taste of power is intoxicating to any soul marked by original sin; it leads to the desire for more power; it transforms public servants into kings — into little gods.

Our pride, however, is misplaced. In uncountable ways, our contemporary culture has drained authority from the individual and bestowed it not upon *persons* so much as upon immense, impersonal *entities*. Without even noticing it, we have surrendered much of our personal authority, ceding to nameless and faceless others the right to tell us how to think, what to value, what to disdain, and how to live our lives.

Our highways are crammed with outrageously expensive SUVs burning untold millions of gallons of costly and polluting fossil fuels. Behind the wheels of most of these vehicles sit people whose driving needs could easily be met by small compact cars, cars that would cost far less and require far less gasoline. Why then, do we insist on buying needlessly wasteful vehicles? We don't know, but we have a vague idea that we ought to; that without a car resembling a battleship, we are somehow less than we could be.

Our political campaigns are endless and brutal. Insults are hurled, ancient misdeeds are revealed in blaring headlines, private events are dragged into the bright light of public scrutiny to be rehashed again and again. The din is tremendous, so deafening that by election day we still haven't noticed that no issues have been discussed, that we are making our choice without information on which to base it, that we are voting in a popularity contest.

"It's all about civil rights," we are told stridently. Then, the accusations begin: "You want to deny others the rights you claim for yourself. You're not inclusive." Feeling heartless, we watch the drive for same-sex marriage move inexorably forward on talk of rights, health insurance, joint ownership, and inheritance; on sorrowful stories of people left bereft after the death of a partner. No mention is made of nature, of the difference between a heterosexual relationship and one between those of the same sex — a difference that once seemed obvious but now, somehow, no longer is, a difference that marks those who mention it as bigots. Children are not an issue; they are either forgotten or are something to be acquired during a quick trip to a fertility clinic or, perhaps, with the help of an obliging friend. Like kittens and puppies, you get them when you want them.

And when you don't want them, they're easily disposed of. Abortion is a right, too. It's even in the Constitution. Hidden for nearly two centuries beneath a comma, it was courageously unearthed by wise lawyers, people who understood that biology had gotten things wrong, that a woman's capacity to bear children is not good, as we had thought, but bad. It's the thing that limits her, that keeps her from achieving parity with men. It must be controlled. Society, they revealed, had also gotten things wrong: abortion was not bad; it was good. It gave women control over their bodies; it allowed them to have high-paying jobs; it allowed them to be as irresponsible as men. Society had for centuries believed that when a woman became pregnant, she became pregnant with the child she would one day bear. This, too, we now know to be wrong; we now know that a woman becomes pregnant with something else, something unimportant that will turn into a child only if you let it. When this transformation occurs depends on whom you talk to and what date best suits the needs of the moment.

What authority is it that turns bad into good and good into bad; that declares a baby to be *not* a baby; that tells us that it is our possessions that give us worth; that deafens us with meaningless chatter? It is an authority behind and beneath the obvious authorities in our world. It is no one thing; it is certainly no one person or group of persons. It is the *zeitgeist*; it is the "they," the culture of which we are all a part. It is a thousand things that are themselves conditioned by a thousand other things. It is a powerful but arbitrary authority, one constantly in flux, shifting and mutating and changing like the tides. But it rules us like a king; it has power over us like a god. It is the kind of authority that is inevitable in every society inhabited by beings who sin.

To be truly human — to bear the divine image — is to recognize this authority as the false god that it is. We must rise above the clamor of the world with its constantly changing ideas and competing demands to find a source of authority that is truth itself. In the Gospel of St. Mark, we read that Jesus "entered the synagogue and taught. And they were astonished at his teaching for he taught them as one who had authority, and not as the scribes" (Mk 1:21-22). In the very next line, Jesus is confronted by a man possessed by an unclean spirit. The spirit is frightening; it convulses the man it inhabits, but it quickly yields to Jesus. As the authority of Christ had complete control over the unclean spirit, so the same Christ can have complete control over the spirit of this world, if we but turn to Him. If we do, we will be able to know truth from falsity, good from bad, those things that have eternal value from the fads of the moment. Like the people in the Gospel of St. Mark, we will say in joy and amazement: "With authority he commands even the unclean spirits, and they obey him" (Mk 1:27).

Quotation for Meditation

We shall be blessed with clear vision if we keep our eyes fixed on Christ, for he, as Paul teaches, is our head, and there is in him no shadow of evil. Saint Paul himself and all who have reached the same heights of sanctity had their eyes fixed on Christ, and so have all who live and move and have their being in him.

As no darkness can be seen by anyone surrounded by light, so no trivialities can capture the attention of anyone who has his eyes on Christ. The man who keeps his eyes upon the head and origin of the whole universe has them on virtue in all its perfections; he has them on truth, on justice, on immortality and on everything else that is good, for Christ is goodness itself.

The wise man, then turns his eyes toward the one who is his head, but the fool gropes in darkness. No one who puts his lamp under a bed instead of on a lampstand will receive any light from it. People are often considered blind and useless when they make the supreme Good their aim and give themselves up to the contemplation of God, but Paul made a boast of this and proclaimed himself a fool for Christ's sake. The reason he said, *We are fools for Christ's sake*, was that his mind was free from all earthly preoccupations. It was as though he said, "We are blind to the life here below because our eyes are raised toward the One who is our head."

— St. Gregory of Nyssa,
as cited in *Christian Prayer,
The Liturgy of the Hours*, 2016

❧ Quiet Time and Then Discussion ❧

Questions for Meditation

1. In what way do I accept the authority of the world around me without question?

2. How have I allowed the authority of the world to usurp the authority of God in my life?

3. How can I best submit my will to the authority of God?

Prayer

Almighty Father, You are the source of all wisdom, the font of all truth. Permit me to hear Your voice above the world's clamor and to follow Your laws at every moment in my life. I ask this, as I ask all things, through Christ, Our Lord. Amen.

Meditation Eleven

Social Justice

READINGS
Matthew 25:31-46;
Catechism of the Catholic Church § 1928-1948

Life is seldom easy. For some, it is exasperatingly difficult. For a few, it is almost horrifying. We rarely see many people who lead lives of horror, but on occasion they emerge from wherever they have been hiding. They appear in front of us, ghastly reminders of how bad things can get, of how forgotten and ignored by others it is possible to become. Usually they wander city streets, although they seldom look as if they're going anywhere. They are never very clean and are often very, very dirty. They seem to like to speak or sing or shout at people — people who are usually not visible to the rest of us. They carry their entire lives in broken supermarket carts or dirty shopping bags. When they confront us, we don't know what to do; we thrust some change or a dollar into their hands; we murmur a prayer for them, and we rush away thanking God that we are not like them, that we have possessions, a home, a family, friends, a life.

It probably doesn't occur to us as we turn our backs on them (just as everyone else has) and search for a place to wash our hands that beneath all the grime and multiple layers of foul-smelling clothes, we have just encountered the image and likeness of God — and fled from it.

And as we flee, we probably don't realize that we are fleeing, as well, from much of what Scripture urges on us, Jesus expects of us, and the Church demands of us. "Seek justice, correct oppression; defend the fatherless, plead for the widow" (Is 1:17), thunders the prophet Isaiah, letting us know just how important to the Lord is the just treatment of those who cannot fend for themselves. Through the words of the prophet Amos, God says:

> "I hate, I despise your feasts, and I take no delight in your solemn assemblies. Even though you offer me your burnt offerings and cereal offerings I will not accept them, and the peace offerings of your fatted beasts I will not look upon. Take away from me the noise of your songs; to the melody of your harps I will not listen. But let justice roll down like waters, and righteousness like an ever-flowing stream."
>
> — Amos 5:21-24

In these disturbing words, we discover God's priorities; we learn that the performance of religious duties is not enough if the poor remain ignored. Praying for the poor is essential, but it is not enough; we must do what we can do.

Jesus raises these prophetic demands to an even higher level. In the Gospel of St. Matthew, He says, "Truly, I say to you, as you did it to one of the least of these my brethren, you did it to me" (Mt 25:40). Here, we are challenged to view everyone not only as our neighbor but also as being as worthy of our love as Christ Himself.

These are difficult demands, and we are greatly tempted to ignore or neglect them. It is much easier to look away, to cross a street, to pass someone by, to roll up a window, to reassure ourselves that we are good Catholics who go to Mass and contribute to charities and follow all the rules well. But it is truly not enough. The words of the prophets — and those of Jesus Himself — urge us to do more, to help the poor, to protect the weak, to feed the starving, to work to ease the discrepancies between the rich and the terribly poor, to bring God's hope to those who bear His image but live forgotten and in despair.

Quotation for Meditation

It is not enough for us to say: "I love God," but I also have to love my neighbor. St. John says that you are a liar if you say you love God and you don't love your neighbor. How can you love God whom you do not see, if you do not love your neighbor whom you see, whom you touch, with whom you live? And so it is very important for us to realize that love, to be true, has to hurt. I must be willing to give whatever it takes not to harm other people and, in fact, to do good to them. This requires that I be willing to give until it hurts. Otherwise, there is not true love in me and I bring injustice, not peace, to those around me.

It hurt Jesus to love us. We have been created in His image for greater things, to love and to be loved. We must "put on Christ" as Scripture tells us. And so, we have been created to love as He loves us. Jesus makes Himself the hungry one, the naked one, the homeless one, the unwanted one, and He says, "You did it to Me." On the last day He will say to those on His right, "Whatever you did to the least of these, you did to Me, and He will also say to those on His left, whatever you neglected to do for the least of these, you neglected to do it for Me."

—Blessed Teresa of Calcutta,
from a speech given at the National Prayer Breakfast,
Washington, DC, February 1994

ᔄᕩ Quiet Time and Then Discussion ᕩᔄ

Questions for Meditation

1. How often have I turned away from those in need?
2. How often have I failed to see someone in desperate circumstances as a person bearing the divine image?
3. What can I do in my own life or in the life of my community or parish to help those who cannot help themselves?

Prayer

Almighty and eternal God, may Your grace enkindle in everyone a love for the many unfortunate people whom poverty and misery reduce to a condition of life unworthy of human beings. Arouse in the hearts of those who call You Father a hunger and thirst for social justice, and for fraternal love in deed and in truth. Grant, O Lord, peace in our days, peace to souls, peace to families, peace to our country, and peace among nations. Amen.

— Pope Pius XII
as cited in *Prayers for Today*, 5

Meditation Twelve

The Moral Law

READINGS
Psalm 119:25-32; Romans 10:4;
Catechism of the Catholic Church § 1949-1986

A basic moral sense is part of the equipment with which we are born, and in this, we can sense the orderliness with which God has endowed His creation. Our entire universe can be thought of as one vast hymn to order. Precise and immutable laws govern the workings of all things in the physical world. Each star, each galaxy, each animal, each amoeba, each atom is a thread in the immeasurable tapestry that is the universe. Each such thread, tightly entwined with the others, has its unique place. If even the smallest one breaks, the entire tapestry is affected and begins to unravel.

In this vast interrelated and interdependent universe stands man. We alone perceive the connectedness of all things around us; we alone perceive that such a wondrous world could not have sprung into existence by chance, that it must find its source in a limitless will, an infinite intelligence. We alone perceive our lives to be governed not merely by physical laws but another law, as well — a subtle law that enables us to discern what is good, to discover those acts that put us in accord with the divine orderliness. This law, which we call the moral law, is every bit as immutable as the law of gravity, and it has been woven into the fabric of our being as firmly as has our DNA. Dr. Francis Collins, who directed the Human Genome Project, calls DNA the "language of God."[2] As a Christian, he would probably agree with us that God speaks every bit as clearly through the moral law.

Have we ever encountered a person with no sense of right and wrong? Are we able to point to someone who is blissfully unaware of the difference between offering a child a spoonful of honey and offering that child a spoonful of arsenic? Our world is unquestionably filled with people who destroy human life, but how many of them would be surprised to learn that there is something wrong in this? A very few among us who suffer from certain severe psychiatric disorders may lack an instinctive awareness of right or wrong — but this is very rare, and we have no trouble understanding it as a medical disorder. We cannot help but think that such people are missing one of life's essential components, and we are tempted to wonder if they can truly be considered persons at all.

In this, we can perceive — however dimly — that the moral law is not an arbitrary system of values, that it is not culturally produced, that it does not vary with the centuries. The moral law is an integral part of the orderliness with which God has blessed His creations. As such, it exists for our benefit; it is one more thing that helps us find our way back to our heavenly Father. As physical laws bestow order on the universe, so the moral law bestows order on our lives as we interact with others. In the moral law, we discover obligation to others and the rules that make relationship possible. We discover how to link our lives to others without discord, to build human societies that are comprised of interconnected lives, that function smoothly and for the advantage of all. Without the moral law, without an objective concept of good and evil, civilization would be impossible, collapsing over and over again into a morass of conflicting values, demands, and desires.

It has often been said that the Ten Commandments are the most basic, most succinct expression of the moral law. We read in the Old Testament that these commandments transformed the children of Israel from a group of quarrelsome ex-slaves — the dregs of ancient Egyptian society — into a kingdom of priests who would bring the word of God to the world and one day give birth to the Messiah, the Christ. The children of Israel not only accepted God's law, they rejoiced in it. They created a religious civilization steeped in God's law, one in which every act was circumscribed by law and made holy by law. Uncounted volumes have been written exploring the staggering intricacies of Jewish religious law. Fortunately for us, as Christians, we are not asked to devote our lives to such a complex system of religious laws. We seek holiness and discern the will of God in other ways. We do, however, have the moral law. We also have the Church as our infallible guide in determining moral behavior. We must, therefore, be fearless in proclaiming the divine truth and orderliness inherent in the moral law to a world that exalts personal values and extols moral relativism, irrespective of the ultimate consequences.

Quotation for Meditation

Christianity tells people to repent and promises them forgiveness. It therefore has nothing (as far as I know) to say to people who do not know they have done anything to repent of and who do not feel that they have any need of forgiveness. It is after you have realised that there is a real Moral Law, and a Power behind the law, and that you have broken that law and put yourself wrong with that Power — it is after all this, and not a moment sooner, that Christianity begins to talk. When you know you are sick, you will listen to the doctor. When you have realised that our position is nearly desperate, you will begin to understand what the Christians are talking about. They offer an explanation of how we got into our present state of both hating goodness and loving it. They offer an explanation of how God can be this impersonal mind at the back of the Moral Law and yet also a Person. They tell you how the demands of this law, which you and I cannot meet, have been met on our behalf, how God Himself becomes man to save man from the disapproval of God.

— C.S. Lewis,
Mere Christianity, 38, 39

～◎ Quiet Time and Then Discussion ◎～

Questions for Meditation

1. How does man's gift of reason enable him to discern the moral law?

2. How should our discernment of the moral law enable us to love others more fully?

3. How does our being made in the image and likeness of God obligate us to follow the moral law?

Prayer

Are You truly the Spirit of freedom in my life, or are You not rather the God of law? Or are You both? Are You perhaps the God of freedom through law? Your laws, which You yourself have given us, are not chains — Your commands are commands of freedom. In their austere and inexorable simplicity they set us free from our own dull narrowness, from the drag of our pitiful, cowardly concupiscence. They awaken in us the freedom of loving You. Amen.

— Karl Rahner
Prayers for a Lifetime, 26

Meditation Thirteen

Grace and Justification

READINGS
Ephesians 2:1-10; Romans 3:21-26; 6:1-11;
Catechism of the Catholic Church § 1987-2029

Left to our own devices, we are as helpless as we are hopeless. Our best intentions regularly come to very little. We try to do good, and from time to time we succeed, but often we fail. We try to stay away from sin but find ourselves in desperate need of Confession over and over again throughout our lives. We try to rid ourselves of faults but find them to be extraordinarily stubborn companions who just won't leave. If we had to achieve our own salvation, heaven would be devoid of humans except for the Blessed Virgin Mary. The rest of us would end up . . . elsewhere.

But our God loves us despite our fallen nature, our sins, and our many limitations, and He does not ask us for things beyond our power. God in Christ opens the gates of salvation to all of us and asks only that we respond to this incredible act of love. He asks only that we accept it humbly into our lives and that we do our best. God graciously and lovingly justifies us, even though we really don't deserve justification. In so doing, He offers sinful humankind unending and unmerited joy. St. Paul explains this best in his letter to the Church at Ephesus. Telling them that we are saved by the limitless grace of God, he writes:

> For by grace you have been saved through faith; and this is not your own doing, it is the gift of God — not because of works, lest any man should boast. For we are his workmanship, created in Christ Jesus for good works, which God prepared beforehand, that we should walk in them.
>
> — Eph 2:8-10

God's grace is made abundantly available to us through the power of the Holy Spirit, and through this grace and power we are justified. The purifying action of God's grace cleanses us from all unrighteousness. Through God's grace, which we receive initially at Baptism and then later through the other sacraments, we are given the opportunity to cast aside our sins — to be forgiven over and over again, as a parent would forgive a child, completely and with overwhelming love.

In Christ, we are justified; in Christ, we are made clean and acceptable. Through His Passion and death, we are made whole. In His dying on Calvary, we are made able to die to sin. In His rising again, we are born to new life as part of His Mystical Body, as one of the branches grafted on to the life-giving vine, the vine who is Christ Himself. From His wounded side flow abundant graces — the Church and the sacraments, grace and healing and justification. All these make us, in the words of St. Paul, a "new creation" (2 Cor 5:17).

Although God doesn't ask us to save ourselves, God does demand that we not be indifferent to His saving acts. It is our profound responsibility to respond to the great outpouring of God's love that gives us new life and new being. It is our duty to cooperate with the graces that God so abundantly bestows upon us, to accept them gratefully and joyfully. These graces give us the power to transform ourselves, to live lives of ongoing conversion, to detach ourselves to a greater and greater degree from sin, to slowly — painfully slowly — become the people we really should be. We must respond; we must take the first step, for God will never infringe on the freedom that He has given us. He makes us free to embrace the new life that we are offered in Christ, or reject it and stay mired in the despair of the dying world in which we spend our earthly lives.

In joy and thanksgiving, we who call ourselves Christian should do all that is in our power to cooperate with God's graces. We who have died with Christ in Baptism should live risen lives — lives of love, compassion, and inner peace, lives that make others who do not know Christ long for what we have been so graciously given. We are as helpless on our own as we are hopeless, but we are not alone; we walk with the Risen Christ and with countless saints who lived before us. We walk as a new creation. We are a new being.

Quotation for Meditation

We Catholics don't use the word justification very often. In fact we sometimes think it is a Protestant word. However, it is very much an important part of Catholic doctrine. In the Catholic teaching of the word, it signifies what God does to us when we make ourselves available to His grace. This is the work of grace, a conversion which happens first, according to our own Lord's proclamation that we must repent because the kingdom of God is at hand. Justification removes us from the life of sin and gives us a righteousness before the Lord. It was merited for us by the suffering and passion of Christ. However, justification goes even beyond that and establishes a certain cooperation between God's grace and our freedom. In many ways justification is a necessary gift because the whole life of grace depends on it as the opening of the soul to God's grace. By justification, we go from death to life; then we need grace to sustain that life within us and to live the life that Christ calls us to.

What is the reason we don't think of justification more often? Perhaps it is because it happened to us very early in our spiritual lives. But we should go back over this mystery and realize the importance and immense gift that has been given to us by this key to the spiritual life and Christian life. We must first believe in Him, before He can become effectively our Savior, and we can only believe in Him because of His gift of grace.

— Fr. Benedict J. Groeschel, C.F.R.,
Retreat given for the Oratory of Divine Love,
November 2004

Quiet Time and Then Discussion

Questions for Meditation

1. What does it mean to be justified?
2. What role do the sacraments play in our justification?
3. What can we do to better cooperate with God's grace in our lives?

Prayer

Save me, Lord, or I shall drown. Life is too difficult; my sins are too onerous, my mistakes are too numerous. I can't manage without You — not even for a second. Send Your grace into my heart, I beg You; wash away my sins and turn me back to You. Do for me what I can't ever hope to do for myself: make me worthy to bear the divine image which I carry — the image that I deface day by day. I am unworthy; make me worthy, I pray, if not for my sake, then for Yours. Amen.

Meditation Fourteen

The Church as Mother and Teacher

❧

READINGS
Matthew 28:18-20; Hebrews 13:7-9;
Catechism of the Catholic Church *§ 2030-2051*

As surely as God is our Father, so the Church is our Mother. And, as every mother loves and guides her children, so Holy Mother Church loves and guides us. She sustains us with the endless graces which flow from her sacraments. She feeds us lovingly in the Eucharist and holds out to us God's forgiveness in the Sacrament of Reconciliation; she offers us strength and support, opening the gates of sanctity for us at every moment in our lives. And when our day on earth is done, it is she who sends us home to our heavenly Father.

As a mother is the path into life for her children, so Holy Mother Church is our path to eternal life. As the *Catechism* declares, "The Church in this world is the sacrament of salvation, the sign and the instrument of the communion of God and men" (*CCC* 780). The graces that God bestows upon the Church burst forth from her, overflowing and pervading the entire world. The Church beckons to all, offering love and salvation to everyone who desires them.

As surely as every mother is the first and most important teacher of her children, so Holy Mother Church is our primary and best teacher. From the Church, we learn the story of our heavenly Father's unending love for us; from her, we learn God's own truth. Through precept and example, the Church teaches us how to live our lives in accordance with the divine law. In short, from our mother, the Church, we learn to be truly human; we learn to be children of God.

As a mother protects her children from harm, so Holy Mother Church protects us. Through preaching and catechesis, her representatives keep us free from error. They show us the way to reform our lives, to better live the morally good life, and direct us in our worship of our heavenly Father. They offer us correction when we are wrong, healing when we are broken, and the assurance of infallible authority when we are confused and uncertain. Without the Church, there could be no priesthood, no sacraments, no Magisterium, no true understanding of what our relationship with God should be. She protects us from giving our allegiance to the false gods the world loves to worship — idols that can lead only to emptiness and despair. In the Church's representatives — the priests, bishops, and especially the Holy Father — we find authentic teachers, authentic pastors, our heavenly Father's true representatives on earth. We find hope, joy, and the way to eternal life, which is Christ Himself.

As surely as a mother is the center of her family, so Holy Mother Church is the center of the Christian community. In and through the Church, we encounter those who thirst for God, those whose lives are marked by holiness. In the Church, we are strengthened by learning of the saints who have come before us, and we attempt as best we can to prepare the way for those who will come after us. In the members of the Church, we see what it is to be a witness for the Lord, and we work to become such witnesses. In the Church — as nowhere else — we meet Christ. We meet Him in the sacraments and in Scripture; we meet Him in the Church itself, for the Church is also the Mystical Body of Christ. As part of the Church, we become part of His Body.

The Church is our mother, our teacher, our true home on earth. We must love her, thank her, revere her, and protect her. At all times, we must pray for her.

Quotation for Meditation

[T]he task of giving an authentic interpretation of the Word of God, whether in its written form or in the form of Tradition has been entrusted to the living teaching office of the Church alone. Its authority in this matter is exercised in the name of Jesus Christ. Yet this Magisterium is not superior to the word of God, but is its servant. It teaches only what has been handed on to it. At the divine command and with the help of the Holy Spirit, it listens to this devotedly, guards it with dedication and expounds it faithfully. All that it proposes for belief as being divinely revealed is drawn from this single deposit of faith.

— *Dei Verbum*, #10

≈ Quiet Time and Then Discussion ≈

Questions for Meditation

1. How does the Church differ from other institutions, including other religious bodies?
2. Why do we know the teachings of the Church to be authentic?
3. How does the Church lead us to Christ?

Prayer

~∾◉

O Jesus, divine Master, I bless and thank Your most sweet heart for the great gift of the Church. She is the mother who instructs us in the truth, guides us on the way to heaven, and communicates supernatural life to us. She continues Your own saving mission here on earth, as Your Mystical Body. She is the ark of salvation; she is infallible, indefectible, catholic. Grant me the grace to love her as You loved and sanctified her in Your blood. May the world know her, may all sheep enter Your fold, may everyone humbly cooperate in Your kingdom.

— Prayer in Thanksgiving for the Gift of the Church
as cited in *The Vatican II Weekday Missal*,
2360-2361

Meditation Fifteen

The Ten Commandments

READINGS

Exodus 20:1-18; Deuteronomy 5:1-27; Matthew 5:14-19;
Catechism of the Catholic Church § 2052-2082

The book of Exodus is the second book of the Bible. It is also one of the greatest and most dramatic rescue stories ever told, complete with heroes, villains, and cliffhangers. At its beginning, the children of Israel are without hope. Marked for extinction, they have been pressed into unendurable slavery by the Egyptian Pharaoh, slavery that by its very cruelty will surely end in their destruction. Everyone has abandoned them, even — it seems — their God, the God who once entered into covenant with their forefather Abraham, the God about whom they have completely forgotten during their 400-year sojourn in Egypt.

But this forgotten God turns out not to be a God who forgets, who breaks His promises, or who abandons His covenants.

When all seems bleakest, this God raises up Moses. In the company of his siblings, Aaron and Miriam, and relying only on the strength of the God of his ancestors, Moses forces the powerful Pharaoh to release the Hebrew slaves. The God of Israel protects His people as they flee their oppressors. He splits the Sea of Reeds for them. He destroys Pharaoh's army for them. He shelters and feeds them at every turn. He promises them a land of milk and honey, far from oppression. And once again, He offers them covenant — this time in the form of the Ten Commandments.

In the forbidding wilderness at Mt. Sinai, God shows His people the way to a new and deepened relationship with Him. As lightning flashes and thunder rumbles, He reveals His commandments to His servant Moses. He does not demand mere sacrifices; He demands of His people things beyond what the Egyptians could ever imagine: they must treat each other as human beings, as people of worth, as children of God — as children of the God who loves them, saves them, and calls them His own.

And, with the revelation of the Ten Commandments at Mt. Sinai, a ragtag band of runaway slaves takes the first step toward becoming a nation. Certainly, this change was not immediate. It must have been a slow, difficult process as the children of Israel, used only to the oppression of pagan Egypt, gradually learned what it meant not to kill, not to take by force what was not theirs, not to deceive, and not to worship anything but the God who was their redeemer. It has been said that one of the many reasons they remained in the wilderness for forty years was that it took that long for these commandments to become part of the fabric of their newly established society. But it so became, and the world began to be transformed.

The Ten Commandments form the basic ethical heritage of Judaism and of Christianity as well. They are a distillation of God's law, the Jewish people's great gift to the world. They form the basis of much of the teaching of our divine Savior, who often showed them to be not just rules to govern our actions but tools we can use to transform our intent, our thinking, our spirituality. By revealing the deeper meanings of the Ten Commandments, He was able to bring people to a more profound understanding of how God intended us to live our lives. For all these reasons and more, we will focus on the Ten Commandments for the next several meditations.

The Ten Commandments, as recorded in the Old Testament, are:

I. I am the Lord your God: you shall not have strange Gods before me.

II. You shall not take the name of the Lord your God in vain.

III. Remember to keep holy the Lord's Day.

IV. Honor your father and your mother.

V. You shall not kill.

VI. You shall not commit adultery.

VII. You shall not steal.

VIII. You shall not bear false witness against your neighbor.

IX. You shall not covet your neighbor's wife.

X. You shall not covet your neighbor's goods.

Quotation for Meditation

Through the Decalogue [God] prepared man for friendship with himself and for harmony with his neighbor. This was to man's advantage, though God needed nothing from man.

This raised man to glory, for it gave him what he did not have, friendship with God. But it brought no advantage to God, for God did not need man's love. Man did not possess the glory of God, nor could he attain it by any other means than through obedience to God. This is why Moses said to the people: "Choose life, that you may live and your descendants too; love the Lord your God, hear his voice and hold fast to him, for this is life for you and length of days."

This was the life that the Lord was preparing man to receive when he spoke in person and gave the words of the Decalogue for all alike to hear. These words remain with us as well; they were extended and amplified through his coming in the flesh but not annulled.

— St. Irenaeus,
as cited in *The Office of Readings*, 391

⁓ Quiet Time and Then Discussion ⁓

Questions for Meditation

1. How does the Decalogue form the basis of Judeo-Christian ethical thought?
2. How does Jesus affirm the importance of the Decalogue?
3. How does Jesus deepen our understanding of the laws contained in the Decalogue?

Prayer

Happy are those whose lives are faultless,
who live according to the law of the Lord.
Happy are those who follow His commands,
Who obey Him with all their heart,
Surely they do no wrong;
They walk in the Lord's ways.
You have given us Your laws,
and told us to obey them faithfully.
How I hope that I shall be faithful
in keeping Your rules!
If I pay attention to all Your commandments,
Then I will not be disappointed.
As I learn Your righteous rulings,
I will praise You with a pure heart.
I will obey Your laws;
don't ever abandon me!

— From Psalm 119
Translated by Fr. Benedict J. Groeschel, C.F.R.

Meditation Sixteen

The First Commandment

⚜

READINGS
Deuteronomy 6:4-9; Matthew 22:34-40;
Catechism of the Catholic Church § 2083-2141

The children of Israel cower at the foot of Mt. Sinai. Smoke envelops everything, making it all but impossible to see. Deafening claps of thunder come one after another, and the sound of a ram's horn, piercing and strident, will not stop. There is so much noise that speech is useless. The people tremble in terror, realizing they are in the presence of a type of majesty that makes the Egyptian Pharaoh from whom they have fled seem puny — and, perhaps, preferable. They know awe as never before. Moses, the one on whom they have depended, has ascended the mountain; he's been swallowed up by the smoke.

This terrifying scene, we are told by the writers of the book of Exodus, is the setting for the reception of the Decalogue, the Ten Commandments. This is the Israelites' first encounter with the God who has redeemed them from Egyptian slavery. They must endure all this to receive the laws that will transform them into a holy people. Such an event is unforgettable; it sears itself into the memory. We might wonder, therefore — what is the point of the First Commandment after the theophany on Mt. Sinai? With the thunder still ringing in their ears, who among the Israelites needed to hear "I am the Lord your God, who brought you out of the land of Egypt, out of the house of bondage. You shall have no other gods before me" (Dt 5:6-7)?

Every one of them, it seems; before Moses could even descend the mountain cradling the twin tablets of the Law in his arms, the children of Israel had already returned to the idolatry of their Egyptian past and were dancing orgiastically around a golden calf — worshiping nothingness while still in the very presence of the Lord.

In this astonishing scene, we see the absolute need for the First Commandment; the importance of striving to keep it first in our lives at all times, reminding ourselves about it when we lie down, when we rise up, and at every moment in between. We frail humans, so weakened by sin, prefer a thousand idolatries to the one true God.

The Protestant theologian Paul Tillich claimed that it is possible to describe faith as "ultimate concern." We are concerned about many things, of course, but the only thing that should concern us ultimately is what is truly ultimate: God. Tillich writes, "Whatever concerns man ultimately becomes God for him."[3] As Catholics, we can find many things to dispute in the theology of Paul Tillich, but we can agree wholeheartedly with the simple but profound truth of these words. We can agree that in allowing ourselves to be ultimately concerned about anything but God, we have lapsed into idolatry. The words of Tillich echo the words of the First Commandment and are a stern warning to keep God first, a demand to avoid making idols of money, fame, power, or any national group. A German who fled the Nazis, Tillich had certainly encountered some of the darkest idolatries of which the human soul is capable.

In the stark words of the First Commandment we discern our primary responsibility: to love, fear, serve, and worship our Creator, to set God before all things at every moment, to live in perfect obedience to the divine will. Often, we fulfill this responsibility no better than did our ancient ancestors in faith at the foot of Mt. Sinai. We are just as prone to reject the One who created us and offers us eternal life, just as eager to bow down to the empty, inert idols the world adores. As Catholics, we know we must turn from our idolatries, as we must turn from all sin. We should see in the first of God's commandments a call to turn to the One who is truly ultimate: a call to examine our lives; to root out the secret idols, the golden calves that hold us in bondage, and replace those idols with the God who has loved us into being.

At the foot of Mt. Sinai, the frightened children of Israel encountered a God they had never known, a God who kept them at a distance and whom they could not comprehend. To them, He was a God of power and might, a fearsome God who issued commands and demanded to be their ultimate concern. At the foot of the altar, we regularly encounter that same God in the Eucharist. Blessed to know Him in ways far deeper than the ancient Israelites ever could, we understand our God to be a God of love, One who offers infinite ways for us to draw closer to Him. If we truly turn to this God, if we truly give Him His rightful place, our lives will become so full, our joys so abundant, that there will be no room for us to put other gods before Him.

Quotation for Meditation

"Yahweh, thy God, is an only God" — this fundamental confession, which forms the background to our creed, making it possible, is in its original sense a renunciation of the surrounding gods. It is a confession in the fullest sense of this word, that is, it is not the registration of one view alongside others but an existential decision. As a renunciation of the gods it also implies the renunciation both of the deification of political powers and the deification of the cosmic [dying and becoming]. If one can say that hunger, love and power are the forces which motivate man, then one can point out, as an extension of the observation, that the three main forms of polytheism are the worship of bread, the worship of love and the idolization of power. All three paths are aberrations; they make absolutes out of what is not in itself the absolute and thereby makes slaves of men.

— Cardinal Joseph Ratzinger (Pope Benedict XVI),
Introduction to Christianity, 73

ᕲ Quiet Time and Then Discussion ᕲ

Questions for Meditation

1. Discuss what it means to fear, serve, and worship God, and why this is an important aspect of God's purpose for mankind.
2. What secret idols do you worship in your own life?
3. What can we do to keep God first in our lives?

Prayer

*Almighty One, heaven and earth are
the work of Your hands.
Eternal One, Your creative will
is the source of all that is.
Father, Your glory fills the whole world.
Who is like You, Eternal God?
Perfect unity,
Undivided trinity,
Gentleness,
Compassion,
God who dwells in our hearts,
God whom the universe cannot contain,
God, beside whom there can be no others.
Let us never forget that You are the first;
You are last; You are the only one. Amen.*

Meditation Seventeen

The Second Commandment

READINGS
Exodus 3:13-18; Deuteronomy 5:11;
Psalm 29; Psalm 96; Acts 4:5-12;
Catechism of the Catholic Church § 2142-2167

A culture in which people did not have names would be unimaginable, and a language that did not overflow with names would be unthinkable. Our names proclaim us to be individuals. Names are bestowed on us with almost sacred care. They distinguish us as being members of our families, descendants of our ancestors, and linked to our ethnic heritage. Things have numbers; people have names. Our names make us known by others as unique people. To call someone by his name is to take the first step toward meeting that person as a person. It is the beginning of relationship. Only a hermit — one who has abandoned human relationships — needs no name.

In the Second Commandment, we are warned, "You shall not take the name of the Lord your God in vain." And this makes perfect sense. If our mere human names are so valuable to us, then how infinitely more precious must be the name of God Himself? "In the name of the Father, and of the Son, and of the Holy Spirit," we say as we begin prayer and as we end it. "Hallowed be Thy name," we say whenever we pray the prayer that Jesus taught us. We recognize these as holy words, and they remind us that the name of God is unique and deserving of reverence and awe. We must not use the name of God lightly. We must not use it to swear falsely. We must not ever turn it into a curse. We are blessed to know the name of Jesus as the human name of God, and we bow our heads at its every mention. In this name of Jesus, we find the name of a person with whom we can be in relationship. Each time we invoke it prayerfully, we open the door again to that relationship with our divine Savior, with the Holy Trinity.

The name of Jesus makes the Second Commandment concrete for us. Here, we have a great advantage over those who lived before the Incarnation and those who have lived since it but have not known Christ. For them, God remains invisible, distant; no images of Him are possible and no name for Him is utterable. In the Old Testament, God is called: *El, Elohim, Shaddai,* and *Adonai.* The first two of these are variations of each other and are generic names that could be applied to any god in an ancient Semitic culture; the third means "the almighty;" the fourth means "my Lord." All these names reveal themselves not to be names at all, but descriptions of godliness or power or sovereignty. Even the tetragrammaton — YHWH, thought to be God's real name — was utterable only by the high priest once each year. It was all but forbidden to the human voice; after the destruction of the Temple, it eventually came to be considered unpronounceable.

Standing before the burning bush, Moses dares to ask the name of God, wanting to know which deity among Egypt's multiplicity of deities will redeem the Israelite slaves. "I AM who I AM," God responds, giving Moses a name that, once again, is not a name (and giving biblical scholars much to ponder). We know what Moses did not: that the God who spoke from the burning bush needed no distinguishing from other gods. That He was the source and sustainer of all, the God who would soon prove the idols of Egypt to be illusion. God reveals much to Moses, and Moses accomplishes much through God's power and favor, but Moses can never truly name the God who speaks to him. And so their relationship, profound as it is, is in some ways less than is offered to us when we call Jesus by name.

The all-powerful God, wrapped in thick smoke and billowing clouds, issues commandments from the heights of Mt. Sinai, and the world trembles in response, vowing never to use the name of this God in vain. As Catholics, we tremble no less than anyone else at the awesomeness of the Sovereign of the Universe, but we are confident, for we know the name of this God to be more than a mere word to use wisely. We know the name of this God to be a person, a person we meet regularly in the Eucharist. In that meeting, we honor the sacred name of God who is Father, Son, and Holy Spirit, and we enter into a relationship that offers eternal life and endless joy.

Quotation for Meditation

Paul teaches us the power of Christ's name when he calls him the power and wisdom of God, our peace, the unapproachable light where God dwells, our expiation and redemption, our great high priest, our paschal sacrifice, our propitiation; when he declares him to be the radiance of God's glory, the very pattern of his nature, the creator of all ages, our spiritual food and drink, the rock and the water, the bedrock of our faith, the cornerstone, the visible image of the invisible God. He goes on to speak of him as the mighty God, the head of his body, the Church, the firstborn of the new creation, the firstfruits of those who have fallen asleep, the firstborn of the dead, the eldest of many brothers; he tells us that Christ is the mediator between God and man, the only-begotten Son crowned with glory and honor, the Lord of glory, the beginning of all things, the king of justice and of peace, the king of the whole universe, ruling a realm that has no limits.

Paul calls Christ by many other titles too numerous to recall here. Their cumulative force will give some conception of the marvelous content of the name "Christ," revealing to us his inexpressible majesty, insofar as our minds and thoughts can comprehend it. Since, by the goodness of God, we who are called "Christians" have been granted the honor of sharing this name... it follows that each of the titles that express its meaning should be clearly reflected in us.

— St. Gregory of Nyssa,
as cited in *The Office of Readings*, 813

➷ Quiet Time and Then Discussion ➷

Questions for Meditation

1. When I think of the name of God, what am I really thinking of?
2. Do I sometimes transgress the Second Commandment without realizing it? What can I do to control my speech to avoid the misuse of the name of God?
3. How can I better give honor to the name of Jesus?

Prayer

Our Father, in Whom is Heaven, holy is Your name!
Lord Jesus Christ, Redeemer of our souls,
holy is Your name!
Holy Spirit, Sustainer and Sanctifier,
holy is Your name!
Holy Trinity, ever-living God, the whole universe
reverberates with the majestic sound of Your name.
In awe and trembling we utter Your name.
In joy and exaltation we sing Your name.
In pain and anguish we call upon Your name.
In doubt and uncertainty we hear Your name
whispered in the silence of our hearts.
Creator of all, lover of souls, You live in holiness
and give meaning to our lives.
May the praise of Your holy name
never depart from our lips. Amen.

The Third Commandment

༠༨༠

READINGS

Genesis 2:1-3; Exodus 31:16-17; Deuteronomy 5:12-15;
Mark 2:27; Revelation 1:10;
Catechism of the Catholic Church § 2168-2195

Holy days of various kinds are common to most religions. Some such observances commemorate historical events, such as the birth of a founder. Others seek to endow seasonal changes with religious meaning. Most holy days occur annually; a few occur with greater frequency. The Sabbath, however, arrives every week, bestowing a special holiness and meaning on every seventh day.

A day of incomparable importance to our Hebrew ancestors in faith, the Sabbath is the only holy day mandated by the Ten Commandments and the one Jewish festival taken up by the Church. "Remember the Sabbath day and keep it holy," the Third Commandment tells us, giving us a profound duty, an obligation that we must carry out — even in our fast-paced, contemporary world. One of God's great gifts to our Jewish ancestors in faith, the Sabbath has become our gift as well. It has been made ours through Christ's life, death, and resurrection.

The book of Exodus tells us, "Six days shall you labor, and do all your work; but on the seventh day is a sabbath to the Lord your God; in it you shall not do any work" (Ex 20:9-10). This command makes the Sabbath an oasis in time, one day out of every seven when we are to try to live in the joy and tranquility of our Creator's world rather than the stress and confusion of ours. The Sabbath should be for us a standard by which we measure our lives — a rule of thumb, a kind of plumb line, something from which many good things flow.

God's gift of the Sabbath helps us to observe the First Commandment. In fact, we might even say that keeping the First Commandment is the reason for the existence of the Third. When we rest from work one day each week and devote that day to quietness, to the Eucharist, and to prayer, we are made to forget the many meaningless distractions that clutter our lives; we become able to focus on our heavenly Father. These commandments, the First and Third, draw our attention solely to God, to the central place God must occupy in our lives, and to the divine order that controls the universe. The Sabbath, properly observed, allows nothing to interfere with the realization that

God is the origin of our existence and our salvation. We must rely on many things if our earthly lives are to continue — food, drink, shelter, money, the help of others. The Third Commandment reminds us that none of these is of primary importance; that ultimately, God alone gives us our existence, and we must give our Creator the primary position in our lives at all times.

The Third Commandment tells us to keep the Sabbath day holy. *Kadosh* is the Hebrew word for "holy," and it is derived from a root that means *to separate, to keep apart*. The Sabbath reminds us that God has separated us from the rest of creation unto Himself, for we alone are created in His image and likeness. Through the death and resurrection of Jesus, God destroys our death, thus separating us further from the dying world in which we spend our earthly existence. We are distinct from the rest of creation, for we are offered eternity rather than a brief moment in time. Through Baptism and the other sacraments, God bestows endless life-giving graces upon us. The Sabbath is a weekly reminder of this never-ending stream of grace; it reminds us that our Creator is the source, sustainer, and sovereign of all.

Saturday, the seventh day, is the day during which God rested after creating the universe. For this reason, it has always been the Sabbath among the Jewish people. For them, the Sabbath begins at sundown on Friday and extends until one hour after sundown on Saturday. It is a time of profound holiness, a time when the presence of God is so palpable, the graces of God so abundant, that those who observe God's commandments are thought to be endowed with a second soul. The eternal part of them, the holy part of them, is thus magnified by the holy Sabbath itself. For the pious Jew, the Sabbath is a time of quiet but intense joy, a moment of unconquerable hope. The Jewish people have undergone uncountable trials and tribulations during their many centuries of existence, and it has often been said that "It was not the Jews who kept the Sabbath; it was the Sabbath that kept the Jews." In this statement, we see the Sabbath as a means by which God protects His chosen people. Thus, the Sabbath is a source of life itself.

As Christians, we celebrate the Sabbath very differently but no less intensely. Our Sabbath, of course, is Sunday — the first, not the last, day of the week. We call this Christian Sabbath the Lord's Day. For the devout Christian, our Sabbath is also a day of unimaginable holiness, for the first day of the week is the day when all things were made new, the day on which Jesus rose from the dead, overcoming sin, destroying the finality of the grave, restoring all that sinful man had lost. As the seventh day represents the completion of creation in the Old Testament, so Sunday in the New Testament is the day when creation bursts forth from God once again, renewing a dying world, redeeming it, filling it with new life, new hope, new holiness. For us, Sunday is the eighth day of creation and the first day of redemption.

The Christian Sabbath is the day given over in a special way to the celebration of the Eucharist, the sacrament of our redemption, the sacrament of new and unending life. As we participate in the Eucharist on the Lord's day, we encounter Christ in an unequaled way. We become partners with Him in our own redemption and in the redemption of all humankind; we join with God in His ongoing work of redemption in our world; and we bring a little closer the moment when the eternal Sabbath will reign, when the peace of God's kingdom will pervade all of existence.

Quotations for Meditation

He who wants to enter the holiness of the day must first lay down the profanity of clattering commerce, of being yoked to toil. He must go away from the screech of dissonant days, from the nervousness and fury of acquisitiveness and the betrayal in embezzling his own life. He must say farewell to manual work and learn to understand that the world has already been created and will survive without the help of man. Six days a week we wrestle with the world, wringing profit from the earth; on the Sabbath we especially care for the seed of eternity planted in the soul. The world has our hands, but our soul belongs to Someone Else. Six days a week we seek to dominate the world, on the seventh day we try to dominate the self.

— Abraham Joshua Heschel
The Sabbath, 11

———

It is right . . . to claim, in the words of a fourth century homily, that "the Lord's Day" is "the lord of days". Those who have received the grace of faith in the Risen Lord cannot fail to grasp the significance of this day of the week with the same deep emotion which led Saint Jerome to say: "Sunday is the day of the Resurrection, it is the day of Christians, it is our day". For Christians, Sunday is "the fundamental feastday", established not only to mark the succession of time but to reveal time's deeper meaning.

— Pope John Paul II, *Dies Domini*

❧ Quiet Time and Then Discussion ❧

Questions for Meditation

1. Think about what it means to rest on the Sabbath. What can we do to increase the holiness of our own observance of the Lord's Day?

2. Discuss the relationship between the First and Third Commandments.

3. What should we do to make our observance of the Lord's Day set the pace for the entire week?

Prayer

Eternal Father, on the first day of the week Your blessed Son rose from the dead, renewing creation, banishing death, and freeing us from our sins. Each week, we recall with thanksgiving this day when all things were made new. Let the first day of the week be for us a day steeped in holiness, a day of joy, a day in which we celebrate Your love, a day of true Sabbath rest. We ask this through Jesus Christ, Our Lord. Amen.

Meditation Nineteen

The Fourth Commandment

READINGS
Genesis 49:28-33, 50:14; Luke 2:41-51; John 19:25-27;
Catechism of the Catholic Church § 2196-2257

Nothing about us makes our existence necessary, yet God creates us anyway. Nothing about us can help our heavenly Father in the slightest; still, He sustains us from instant to instant, His divine will keeping us from slipping into the nothingness from which we were called forth at our conception. As Father, Son, and Holy Spirit, God exists eternally — in perfect love; in unmarred relationship; in unblemished happiness. God lacks nothing; therefore His ongoing acts of creation do not find their origin in any kind of need. Instead, God creates out of sheer love, a love so strong that it gives birth to a universe, to innumerable worlds, to uncountable creatures, to humankind, to each and every one of us.

And God urges us to join Him in His acts of creation, to be a little bit like Him. "Be fruitful and multiply," God says to Adam and Eve, knowing full well the problems that humankind will cause but (amazingly) loving us all anyway. Out of love, Adam and Eve give birth — not to a universe but to a child, and not out of nothingness, as God creates, but out of their own bodies, their very beings. Although Scripture is silent on the matter, it's probably safe to say that God looked on this new little creation and saw that it was good . . . even though He knew this child, Cain, would one day kill.

Parenthood that flows from real and unselfish love is a gift from God, a source of holiness, of life and joy, a way of joining our human creativity to the divine creativity. Parents are the first reflection of God to their offspring, our heavenly Father's initial self-revelation to a child. A tiny baby, held tenderly and protectively in his mother's arms, becomes aware of the existence of what he will one day learn to call love — the love of which God is the ultimate source. He understands on some level that the world is not cold and forbidding, that it radiates warmth and caring. This is a lesson that, once learned, becomes a wellspring of hope for a lifetime, a constant reminder that the source of such a world must be compassionate.

To conceive a child is to invite the unknown into one's life. It is to accept a radical change in the focus of one's existence, to be thrust into relationship with an unknown person, to welcome that person with love, no matter what the consequences. In these early days of the twenty-first century, no one needs to conceive a child, and many take great pains to avoid it. Many think that a relationship with a spouse is enough, that there is no reason to invite another into their private world. But those who are open to new life act like God, who creates us all out of love, despite the completion and perfection of His existence and in the full awareness that we will fall short of His desires for us. In such parents, the image and likeness of God burns brightly.

Parenthood confers breathtaking responsibilities. A child, helpless and vulnerable, can do nothing for his parents; his dependence on them is total and continues for years. Our dependence on God is total as well, and continues forever. In the loving and selfless care of children by their parents, we see a reflection of the image and likeness of God. A child does nothing to receive his parents' care except to *be*, but that is enough — as it is enough that by the mere fact of our existence, we are constantly in the care of our heavenly Father.

Parenthood opens the door to heartbreak. All parents make a thousand mistakes; children, once grown, often disappoint and frustrate, sometimes seeming not to be the people their parents thought them to be. Yet they are still loved and forgiven, over and over again. God sees the truth about His human creations — that they are good, despite the overwhelming evidence to the contrary. Parents must sometimes struggle to believe this fact.

If all this is the case, then how could there not be one among the Ten Commandments that tells us to "honor your father and your mother"?

Quotation for Meditation

The observance of the Fourth Commandment within the family or even in relation to legitimate authority outside the family is something that has tended to go by the wayside in modern society. This is partially due to false and incorrect psychology and a misunderstanding of what the responsibilities of parents and children are. Unfortunately, we live in a society where large numbers of people, possibly the majority, have no concept of respect or reverence for the family and for parents and parent surrogates. However, there are some bright signs on the horizon. More and more real families are beginning to recognize that the proper observance of the family authority and family discipline are essential. The place to start is for those in charge, those in parental roles or responsible roles, to fulfill their duties with love, kindness, and firmness when it is necessary.

It is unfortunate that some people appear to be living with a negative attitude toward authority. This can come either from a dysfunctional experience in childhood or perhaps from the influence of evil, either through the media or by the suggestion of the Evil One. It is not to be overlooked that Jesus went down to Nazareth and was subject to Joseph and Mary, who were both, in relation to Jesus, creatures. We find that although from a Godly position they are subject to Him, as His earthly parental figures He was respectful to them. In observing the posture that Jesus takes with Mary and Joseph, how much more should we accept opportunities to be respectful to parents and others in authority.

— Fr. Benedict J. Groeschel, C.F.R.,
Retreat given for the Oratory of Divine Love,
January 2005

⊰ Quiet Time and Then Discussion ⊱

Questions for Meditation

1. How does the relationship between a parent and a child reflect the relationship between God and His human creation?

2. Discuss how parents can show God's love to their children.

3. Discuss what it means to honor someone and offer ways we can show honor to those in legitimate authority.

Prayer

Lord Jesus Christ, You gave us a marvelous example of obedience to and dependence on parents in Your own earthly life. That the Son of God should be subject to human beings is, in itself, mysterious and marvelous. Having given us this good example, help us to show respect to parents and parent figures, to those on whom we have depended at any point during our lives, and if they are dead and gone, that we will have the generosity and gratitude to pray for them on their journey into eternal life. We pray to You, O Christ, Our Lord. Amen.

— Fr. Benedict J. Groeschel, C.F.R.

The Fifth Commandment

Part I: Human Life Is Sacred

READINGS
Matthew 5:21-26; 26:47-52;
Catechism of the Catholic Church § 2258-2283

You shall not kill, says the Fifth Commandment, forcefully reminding us that all life is sacred, that all life is a gift from God, a gift of love. It is the duty of every Christian always to proclaim and uphold the sacredness of all life, especially the unique value of human life — the one form of life that bears the image and likeness of its Creator. Each person is a singular creation of our heavenly Father, a creation — a life — never to be repeated. Because of this uniqueness, each of us has the potential to contribute to the society in which we live in a way that no one else ever could. Each of us is different, yet all of us are bound together by a common humanity, and this humanity, too, is an unmerited gift graciously bestowed upon us by God.

Thus, we can say that from the Christian perspective, our lives are not really our own but have been lent to us by our heavenly Father for His purposes; thus, we can also say that each life possesses a deep and wondrous dignity. Not one life has ever entered human existence except through the will of God. Our Creator alone has the final say about our lives. Our respect for human life, therefore, reflects in a very direct way our respect for God. With this in mind, we are always aware that we do not have the right to destroy a human life, nor may we attempt to bring new human life into existence in ways that are contrary to the will of our heavenly Father. Such acts are seriously sinful; they ignore the ultimate value inherent in human life, demeaning it and denying its unique value, its sanctity.

Contemporary culture — often, and aptly, called the culture of death — is so far removed from an awareness of God that we who live within it have dulled our consciences, overlooked the sacredness of God's human creation, and tried to take upon ourselves authority over human life. This has led only to tragedy and untold sins against the Fifth Commandment.

The 1973 Supreme Court decision in the *Roe v. Wade* case bears this out. This decision, which permitted abortion virtually on demand, initiated a holocaust which continues unabated to this day. Even Christians have been so influenced by the culture of death that many of us ignore or even condone this tragic slaughter of innocents. Every woman has the right to control her own body, we are told — and, in most cases, this is true. But the right to control one's body can never confer the right to supersede the natural and moral laws established by God. Control over one's body can never bestow the right to destroy another human life. If we can kill the unborn without a second thought, why is it difficult to imagine killing the infirm, the elderly, or anyone else whose life has become inconvenient for us?

The hope with which Christians must live is that no matter how bad things may seem, no matter how the Fifth Commandment is flouted in our own time, in God's own time the Holy Spirit will prevail. We read in St. Paul's Letter to the Romans:

> Law came in, to increase the trespass; but where sin increased, grace abounded all the more, so that, as sin reigned in death, grace also might reign through righteousness to eternal life through Jesus Christ our Lord.
>
> — Rom 5:20-21

Oratorians — and all other devout Christians — must speak boldly, with the voice of the Church, to the culture of death. We must become voices crying out in the wilderness. We must pray that the Holy Spirit will inspire the Church to redouble Her efforts against the forces of death. The Gospel of St. Matthew tells us:

> "You are the light of the world. A city set on a hill cannot be hid. Nor do men light a lamp and put it under a bushel, but on a stand, and it gives light to all in the house. Let your light so shine before men, that they may see your good works and give glory to your Father who is in heaven."
>
> — Mt 5:14-16

It is only light that enables us to see, for light obliterates the darkness that obscures our vision. We must truly become the light of the world, the light that banishes the darkness of sin, the light that exposes the truth — that every human life is a gift of God, that every human life is sacred.

Quotation for Meditation

If you ask the average person on the street in the U.S.A. if we have respect for human life, they would certainly say, "Yes." They would think of our country as a law-abiding country that protects the innocent and the defenseless. But is that true? As a result of the *Roe v. Wade* decision in 1973, we have now killed more innocent and defenseless people than were killed at the hands of Hitler's Nazis during the Second World War.

Mother Teresa summed this up very well when she said that no nation that kills its own children can survive. We Oratorians need to be messengers of peace. We need to speak for peace on the international level, national level, local level, and in our families and among our friends and even in the Church. . . .

We Oratorians have to stand out as models of peace and speak against any abuse of human life or destruction of human life. We should be known as those who under all circumstances ask for and demand the protection of human life. If you need a model for this, there is always St. Francis, but an even better model is Our Lord Jesus Christ.

> — Fr. Benedict J. Groeschel, C.F.R.,
> Retreat given for the Oratory of Divine Love,
> January 2005

≈ Quiet Time and Then Discussion ≈

Questions for Meditation

1. Is the destruction of human life different from the destruction of other kinds of life? If so, how?
2. Does anyone ever have the authority to take a human life?
3. Are there limits to the control we may exercise over our own bodies? If so, what are they?

Prayer

Eternal Father, You are a God who delights in life, and You fill our world with countless living things. Give us the grace, we beseech You, to revere Your gift of life, wherever we encounter it, to see Your power and Your love made manifest in every living being.

May we never destroy life of any kind unnecessarily, and may we never fail to recognize the unique sacredness inherent in every human life, the one form of life You create in Your holy image. We ask this through Christ, Our Lord. Amen.

Meditation Twenty-One

The Fifth Commandment
Part II: Respect for the Dignity of Persons

READINGS
Genesis 4:8-16; Isaiah 2:3-5; Matthew 5:9;
Catechism of the Catholic Church *§ 2284-2330*

Most of us will never kill anyone; therefore, the Fifth Commandment is nothing to be concerned about — or so we may think. But over many centuries, the Church has discovered that hidden behind the simple and seemingly direct admonition of the Fifth Commandment are a host of subtleties. A thousand human acts fall far short of murder but spring from the same source within us as the desire to kill. Many acts do not destroy life but injure, limit, or insult it. It is these that make this commandment so important for all of us — we, who would never dream of spilling a drop of another's blood.

The Church clearly reminds us that all willful injury inflicted on others is a sin against the Fifth Commandment, that we may not harm anyone for any purpose. It also reminds us that there are many ways to hurt another, ways that are unrelated to doing damage to that person's body. Thus, we are made aware that things are not as easy as we thought, that we might bear more guilt than we ever expected, for we learn from the Church that to avoid sins against the Fifth Commandment, we must have respect for the dignity of all persons at all times.

"Am I my brother's keeper?" Cain demands indignantly — after committing the first murder, the first sin against the Fifth Commandment (Gen 4:9). In some ways, this is the question we all ask in our relationships with others. The *Catechism,* in its careful explication of the Faith, answers this question for us as part of its discussion of the Fifth Commandment. The answer is a resounding "Yes!"

We may not be passive bystanders where other human beings are concerned. It is not enough merely to do them no harm; we must take an active role in the well-being of both their bodies and their souls. We may do nothing that may lead another to sin, for sin can lead to eternal death, certainly a sin against the Fifth Commandment. We must have concern for the health of others; if we do not, and because of our indifference they fall ill or even die, we have offended God and transgressed the Fifth Commandment. We must be extremely careful in our use of drugs, alcohol, food, and tobacco, for the misuse of any or all of these can lead to injury — and that, too, is a sin against the Fifth Commandment. We must control our anger and desire for revenge, for these regularly lead to sins against the Fifth Commandment. We must reject all hatred; we must work for the avoidance of war; we must work for the physical and spiritual good of all. If we don't, we may slide by neglect into sins against the Fifth Commandment.

There have been untold acts of violence in the history of the human race, countless transgressions of God's command not to kill, not to injure, not to harm. We must all turn inward and examine our own souls to discover in what ways we have fallen short, and we must never for a moment forget that just because we have not followed in the footsteps of Cain and shed the blood of another that the fifth of God's commandments has nothing to say to us.

Quotation for Meditation

Today there is an inescapable duty to make ourselves the neighbor of every man, no matter who he is, and if we meet him, to come to his aid in a positive way, whether he is an aged person abandoned by all, a foreign worker despised without reason, a refugee, an illegitimate child wrongly suffering for a sin he did not commit, or a starving human being who awakens our conscience by calling to mind the words of Christ: "As you did it to one of the least of these my brethren, you did it to me" (Mt 25:40).

The varieties of crime are numerous: all offenses against life itself, such as murder, genocide, abortion, euthanasia and willful suicide; all violations of the integrity of the human person such as mutilation, physical and mental torture, undue psychological pressures; all offenses against human dignity, such as subhuman living conditions, arbitrary imprisonment, deportation, slavery, prostitution, the selling of women and children, degrading working conditions where men are treated as mere tools for profit rather than free and responsible persons; all these and the like are criminal: they poison civilization; and they debase the perpetrators more then the victims and militate against the honor of the creator.

— *Gaudium et Spes*, #27

◈ Quiet Time and Then Discussion ◈

Questions for Meditation

1. In what sense is each of us our brother's keeper?
2. What are some common sins against the Fifth Commandment of which we all may be guilty?
3. Discuss how we can work to decrease the violence in our world.

Prayer

Loving Father, giver of all life, we praise You for the mystery and beauty of all creation, especially the way You have created us in Your own image. Deepen our respect for Your presence in every human person from the first moment of conception until the last natural breath. According to Your will, O Lord, use us as Your instruments to bring about the conversion of all who do not yet share our vision or commitment to the dignity of the life of the unborn and the dying, the chronically ill, the disabled, and migrants. Make us instruments of Your peace and keep us all from the evils of war and violence. We ask all this through Christ, Our Lord. Amen.

Meditation Twenty-Two

The Sixth Commandment
Part I: "Male and Female He Created Them . . ."

❧

READINGS
Genesis 1:26-31; Matthew 5:27-28; 19:3-9;
Catechism of the Catholic Church § 2331-2336

Sexuality is one of the many gifts that our Creator has bestowed upon us. The difference between the sexes, their complementarity, enables us to love deeply and fully in a way that otherwise would not be possible. It enables us to understand that as long as we remain alone, we are not quite complete. It gives us the opportunity to perceive that in the deep love of another — one who is like us, yet still different from us — we can find our wholeness, we can discover our happiness. It allows us to perceive mystery, to enter the world of the other, the one whom we can encounter completely but never become, the one who is as close to us as our own breathing, yet always different. It allows us to participate in creation. Through sexuality we bring new and unique life into the world; out of our own lives we create new life and prepare the way for new souls.

Sexuality is an astounding gift, one that should amaze us, humble us, and fill us with great awe. The psalmists sang of such gifts, and we still repeat their words today:

> I praise thee, for thou art fearful and wonderful. Wonderful are thy works! Thou knowest me right well; my frame was not hidden from thee, when I was being made in secret, intricately wrought in the depths of the earth. Thy eyes beheld my unformed substance; in thy book were written, every one of them, the days that were formed for me when as yet there was none of them. How precious to me are thy thoughts, O God!
>
> — Ps 139:14-17

As we reflect on our heavenly Father's creation of mankind — two equal sexes, each made in the divine image — we should sing in ecstatic praise, just as the psalmists did. We should never stop praising and thanking the God who made us, alone of all creation, to be not just male and female, but simultaneously physical and spiritual beings. Like the other creatures of the earth, we are a physical body; like the angels themselves, we are spirit. Unlike all, we are both. And we are eternal. The soul our God has given us is everlasting, and the body that seems so perishable will one day be raised as Christ was raised. At that moment, we will finally be the persons we were meant to be from the beginning; we will be a perfect union of the physical and the spiritual. The many forces that pull us in a thousand directions will become nothing, for we will no longer be divided; we will be one.

God has given every man and woman the gift of the ability to love, and every man and woman has been given the gift of his or her sexual identity. This identity is one of the deepest parts of us and should be something in which we rejoice. It is a gift we have received, and it is something we are, in turn, expected to bestow upon another as a gift. In marriage, the sexes complement each other and fulfill each other. Together they form a unity that can be said to reflect (in a very imperfect way) the unity of the Trinity itself, in which each member enjoys perfect unity with the others yet remains unique. The world would be very dull and boring without the difference between the sexes, their oppositeness and complementarity.

The confusion growing among men and women in many societies regarding sexuality results, to a great degree, from a lack of appreciation of the different qualities of each sex. Many young people in our society have been brought up to believe that no such difference really exists — that anything that appears to be a difference is simply culturally produced. Many people even believe that sexual preference is unrelated to one's biological sex.

Such a view clearly ignores the obvious and leads only to greater and greater confusion.

The truth is that the sexes are similar and yet unique. Sacred Scripture, as always, can be used to find a standard that is not only workable but holy. In the book of Genesis, we read, "So God created man in his own image, in the image of God he created him; male and female he created them" (Gen 1:27). What's so hard about that?

Quotation for Meditation

I do not understand why some people are saying that women and men are exactly the same, and are denying the beautiful differences between men and women. All God's gifts are good, but they are not all the same. As I often say to people who tell me that they would like to serve the poor as I do, "What I can do, you cannot. What you can do, I cannot. But together we can do something beautiful for God." It is just this way with the differences between women and men.

God has created each one of us, every human being, for greater things — to love and to be loved. But why did God make some of us men and others women? Because a woman's love is one image of the love of God, and a man's love is another image of God's love. Both are created to love, but each in a different way.

Woman and man complete each other, and together show forth God's love more fully than either can do it alone.

— Blessed Teresa of Calcutta, Message to the Fourth International Women's Conference in Beijing, September 1995

✆ Quiet Time and Then Discussion ✆

Questions for Meditation

1. How does God's creation of humankind in two sexes show His great love for us?
2. Discuss how our contemporary culture tends to blur the lines between the sexes.
3. How does God's creation of humankind in two sexes allow us to transcend our solitariness in a unique way?

Prayer

Father, source of endless joy, You create us as male and female: each equally human, each bearing Your image and likeness, each very different from the other. We thank You for the gift of sexuality, for the unique love that You enkindle between man and woman, and for the possibility of new and holy life issuing from that love. Grant us the grace to keep holy this great gift, to see it as part of Your plan of creation, to give honor to You and each other through chaste and loving relationships. We ask this through Christ, Our Lord. Amen.

Meditation Twenty-Three

The Sixth Commandment
Part II: The Vocation to Chastity

READINGS
Genesis 2:24; Matthew 19:6; Titus 2:1-10; Galatians 5:16-25;
Catechism of the Catholic Church § 2337-2359

In our sex-obsessed culture, chastity is a much misunderstood word, a term that seems to belong to the remote past, to a less enlightened moment in history. Today, the mere mention of chastity evokes outright laughter or at least a knowing smile. To many, this word implies impossible, unnatural — even harmful — austerities. Our culture has jettisoned chastity and has proudly announced that the world is a better place for it.

But as we look around us, we cannot avoid drawing other conclusions. We are forced to admit that the disposal of chastity has resulted in a host of ills: abortion on demand, fatherless families, endless divorces, uncountable teenage pregnancies, and numerous diseases, to name but a few. Perhaps, then, our culture didn't quite understand what it was doing when it consigned the virtue of chastity to the unenlightened past. Perhaps we didn't realize that chastity is not simply the frightened avoidance of all things sexual; it is instead, a way of honoring and making holy the sexual aspect of our lives, a way of making sexuality fully human, fully appropriate, steeped in dignity and genuine love. For what our culture simply cannot grasp is that a loving married couple, leading lives of intense intimacy, are being just as chaste as anyone who ever inhabited the cloister.

In the words of the *Catechism*, "Chastity means the successful integration of sexuality within the person and thus the inner unity of man in his bodily and spiritual being" (*CCC* 2337). In other words, chastity helps us to become whole. Without chastity, we remain divided, pulled (sometimes violently) in different directions by our physical desires. This sad state of affairs saturates the media and popular literature of our time. Think of the numberless movies and novels that have depicted characters driven by one sexual obsession or another until they destroy all that is meaningful in their lives.

God's gift of sexuality enables us to participate in creation, but if the virtue of chastity eludes us, if we have not fully integrated our sexuality into our lives, this gift can be deformed into a source of destruction instead. Without chastity, relationships will be wounded as lust becomes entangled with love. Families will be torn apart with infidelities. We will claim to love another, while treating the person as an object to be possessed, a mere means of obtaining pleasure or gratification. These instances illustrate how we need chastity — how it enables us to meet others as people deserving of respect.

It doesn't matter if we are married, single, or widowed; each of us is called to strive for that inner unity that chastity allows us. The expression of chastity, of course, differs according to our state of life. Those who are unmarried are called to respect their own dignity as persons and the dignity of others by refraining from sexual activity. Those who are married are called to make of themselves and their sexuality gifts to their spouses, to share not just physical intimacy but an intimacy that is emotional and spiritual and so saturated with love that it is open to the creation of new life. Thus the virtue of chastity, properly understood, encourages us to live lives of true dignity, lives of authentic love. It is one of the many things that help us to become the people God created us to be.

The world in which we live believes chastity to be an impossibility. We hear every day that indulgence in any and all forms of sexuality is normal, unavoidable, harmless, and even healthy. As Catholics, we strive to live our lives on a plane higher than this. We strive to transform our sexuality from a mere fact of biology to a sacred aspect of our lives; we try to follow the will of God as it leads us down the difficult but beautiful road of chastity to a life of wholeness and true holiness.

Quotation for Meditation

As we strive in life to be Christ's disciples, we come to realize that we do not in fact first love God; He first loves us. Chastity in married or single life is one of several spiritual struggles which reveal Christ's personal love for the individual. Patience and forgiveness are rooted in the long battle to be chaste. As we grow more and more chaste, we come to recognize Christ as the source of a spiritual delight that captivates our heart, mind, soul, and spirit.

It is important to note that the freedom of thought and feeling which comes to the chaste may open wells of repressed desire and feeling. The individual may then have to face unsuspected impulses and temptations; he or she may walk along cliffs of temptation and slip into chasms of desire. It is then that the gifts of the Holy Spirit will come to rescue the traveler and carry him on.

For married and single, following God's law and the way of the Gospel leads to a blessedness that nothing else can bring. Unexpected forces of grace come into play as the person is drawn to the Divine, and the two embrace. The individual is not lost, but transformed. Even in the dark night that follows substantive spiritual progress, the pure of heart receive and respond to the gifts of the Holy Spirit. At that stage of the spiritual life, it is the gift of courage, or fortitude, that is at work in the soul. The person is able to go beyond his or her strength, and with conscious control, to integrate long-buried, irrational forces. And out of that dark conflict which, according to the saints, accompanies every step of the spiritual journey, there comes the realization that the pure of heart do indeed see God.

— Fr. Benedict J. Groeschel, C.F.R.,
The Courage to Be Chaste, 108

ᘒ Quiet Time and Then Discussion ᘒ

Questions for Meditation

1. How can one persevere in the chaste life?
2. Discuss the importance of chastity for those who are single, married, and widowed.
3. How does the struggle for chastity help us to become better followers of Christ?

Prayer

Dearest Jesus!

I know well that every perfect gift, and above all others that of chastity, depends upon the most powerful assistance of Your providence, and that without You, a creature can do nothing.

Therefore, I pray that You defend, with Your grace, the gift of chastity and purity in my soul as well as my body. And if I have ever received through my senses any impression that could stain my chastity and purity, I ask You, who are the supreme Lord of all my powers, to take it from me, so that I may with a clean heart advance in Your love and service, offering myself chaste all the days of my life on the most pure altar of Your divinity. Amen.

— St. Thomas Aquinas

Meditation Twenty-Four

The Sixth Commandment
Part III: The Love of Husband and Wife

READINGS
Genesis 2:15-25; Tobit 8:4-9; 1 Corinthians 13:1-13;
Catechism of the Catholic Church § 2360-2379

God is love, and all His creative acts are rooted in love. The vast universe exists only because divine love has called it into being. We continue to exist only because God's love — constantly coursing through us — holds us in the web of being from instant to instant, shielding us from nothingness, protecting us from being swallowed up by nonbeing. God's human creation is the great beneficiary of divine love, receiving uncountable gifts of love from our Creator at every moment, gifts that make us human, that set us apart from the rest of creation, awesome gifts that enable us to become "little less than God" (Ps 8:5). Among the greatest of these is the ability to love others as God loves us. If we are alone, we are incomplete, for the God who lives in eternal relationship desires that we, too, live in relationship. He has implanted in each of us the need to love, the yearning to share ourselves on a very deep level with another, the ability to form relationships, to perceive in others the divine spark that we sense in ourselves. In relationship, we emerge from our solitude and become more fully human.

Holiness can attach to countless types of human relationships, but in the divine plan there is one relationship which partakes of a special and unique holiness: the relationship that enables us to participate in God's ongoing act of creation — the relationship between husband and wife.

In sacred Scripture, we read, "Therefore a man leaves his father and his mother and cleaves to his wife, and they become one flesh" (Gen 2:24). Here, we are clearly shown the unique quality that characterizes the love between a husband and a wife. It is a love so profound that it enables them to transcend their aloneness, their solitude, completely; to actually "become one flesh." It enables them to become as close to each other as they are close to themselves. This is the relationship that God has ordained to surpass others, to banish estrangement, the relationship in which it is possible to meet another so perfectly that no distance remains at all. This is the relationship that actually reflects the divine reality. As Father, Son, and Holy Spirit flourish as individuals joined in perfect, loving unity, so husband and wife achieve a unity of love that erases all barriers while simultaneously sacrificing nothing of their uniqueness. As husband and wife, two people can achieve a relationship that is more than relationship; it is really communion, and in this communion, they enter a new and more expansive understanding of "self," an understanding that points them directly to God.

The love between husband and wife is a love so intense that it cannot be hoarded. It naturally opens itself to others, becoming the love that creates. As God creates out of love, so the husband and wife bring new life — new creations — into the world out of love. A child is not simply the living symbol of the communion between the husband and wife; the child *is* that communion, that perfect union of both his parents, the union that is love and life simultaneously. The child is the eternal incarnation of that love. The child passes that love along to his children, and their children, and their children's children, keeping that love from slipping into nonbeing . . . passing it along with the image of God, joining human love at its fullest with the divine love that gives life to all.

Quotation for Meditation

We read in Genesis that Rebecca being barren, Isaac entreated the Lord for her, and his prayer was granted

(Gen 25:21). There is no union so precious and so fruitful between husband and wife as that of holy devotion, in which they should mutually lead and sustain each other. There are some fruits, such as the quince, which are uneatable except when preserved, owing to their bitterness, and others such as the apricot and cherry, which are so delicate they cannot be kept except that they are preserved. So wives should endeavor to soften their husbands with sugar of devotion, for without it man is but a rough, harsh being; and husbands should encourage their wives in devotion, for without it a woman is weak and frail. St. Paul says that "the unbelieving husband is sanctified by the believing wife and the unbelieving wife is sanctified by the believing husband" (1 Cor. 7:14). Because in the close union of matrimony one may guide the other to virtue. But that is a truly blessed state in which the faithful husband and wife sanctify one another in the sincere fear of the Lord.

— St. Francis de Sales,
Introduction to the Devout Life, 233

ᔐ Quiet Time and Then Discussion ᔑ

Questions for Meditation

1. How does the love between a husband and a wife differ from other loving relationships?

2. How does the love between a husband and a wife allow them to reflect the divine love in a special way?

3. Why must the love between a husband and a wife be open to new life if it is to be authentic love?

Prayer

Almighty and Eternal Father, You created man in love to share Your divine love. We see his high destiny in the love of husband and wife. Love is man's origin, love is his constant calling, love is his fulfillment in heaven. The love of man and woman is made holy in the sacrament of marriage. Grant that those so united may live so perfectly in Your love that they become for us living signs of the love that mends all brokenness, overcomes all estrangement, and heals all wounds. Amen.

— Adapted from the Rite of Marriage

Meditation Twenty-Five

The Sixth Commandment
Part IV: Offenses against the Dignity of Marriage
Section I: Adultery

READINGS
Leviticus 18:7-20; Jeremiah 5:7-9; 13:27; 1 Corinthians 7:10-11;
Catechism of the Catholic Church § 2380-2400

Adultery is betrayal, and every adulterer betrays at least three times. He betrays his spouse, to whom he has pledged himself exclusively; God, before whom he has solemnly promised to honor the holiness, the sacramentality, of marriage; and himself, by choosing to sin profoundly and obscuring the image of God, which he bears. Adultery is corrosive. It eats away at relationships, bit by bit destroying trust and replacing it with suspicion. Adultery mocks love, for it declares lust superior to love and momentary pleasure more desirable than a lifetime of relationship. Adultery destroys families, ripping children from their parents and teaching them to hate the very people they should most love. Adultery transmutes happiness into grief and community into isolation.

Yet adultery is one of the great pastimes of our culture. It has come to be considered commonplace, almost the new norm. Once considered a reprehensible act, something to be painstakingly concealed and emphatically denied, adultery has lost its status as sin. There is little shame in adultery now. At times it's almost a badge of honor, proclaiming the adulterer to be one not confined by the stultifying rules of society but a free spirit who responds to something higher — the needs of the self. Adultery has become entertainment: our movies and novels glorify it; we laugh at it heartily during prime-time situation comedies. The multiple adulteries of celebrities provide us endless fascination and give us the wonderful opportunity to mix prurience with hero worship.

None of this will change. None of it can change, because adultery will always be strong as long as its holy opposite is weak, and what institution is weaker in our society than the institution — the sacrament — of marriage? The sacramentality of marriage is forgotten; the permanence of marriage has become but one option among many; the totality of self-giving in a real marriage is deemed impossible. The sacred dimension of marriage is so obscured that we can no longer even perceive it. Marriage today is a simple contract, one that can be voided at any moment, one that is being opened to couples of the same sex, and soon — possibly — to groups of three or more. With marriage so diminished, what can be so wrong with adultery? When marriage is a mere technicality, then adultery is one as well.

The betrayal that is adultery tears at the fabric of our society, destroying families every day. As Catholics, we must work against this by proclaiming the sacred union that is marriage, by teaching our children the true nature of marriage — which is infinitely deeper than a mere contract. We must show through example that God is present in a special way in every real sacramental marriage. We must reveal through our own lives that marriage is a living symbol of Christ's intense love for His Church. Only then will the sixth of God's commandments become real in our lives again.

Quotation for Meditation

The central concept of Covenant allows us to understand the meaning of a marriage. It also leads us to a fuller understanding of the meaning of sexual activity within a marriage. Why is it that people do not, in fact, have the "right" to have consensual sex with any other adult they wish? Why is it that sexual activity only belongs within the province of marriage? It is because of the irrevocable gift of self that sexual activity inherently entails and this can only happen in a covenantal relationship. To put it very simply, once we have given ourselves to another person, we are no longer available to give ourselves to anyone else! This total self-giving can only make sense in the context of a permanent relationship. This is not merely a religious argument; this is demonstrated in the makeup of our very bodies and readily understood by anyone truly honest or prudent enough to reflect upon human experience. Sexual intimacy automatically generates a certain degree of relational intimacy on the emotional and spiritual levels. To abuse that intimacy generates a unique kind of hurt — not (only) because God's will for our lives has been ignored, but also because of the very meaning of human identity.

— Christopher P. Klofft, S.T.D.,
Living the Love Story, 113, 114

✎ Quiet Time and Then Discussion ✎

Questions for Meditation
1. Discuss why adultery has become so common in our society.
2. Why is the betrayal of a spouse more profoundly damaging than other forms of betrayal?
3. Discuss ways in which marriage can be strengthened in our society.

Prayer

Heavenly Father,
through the intercession of the Holy Family,
help us to treasure the gift of marriage
*   that reflects the love of Christ for the Church,*
where the self-giving love of husband and wife
unites them more perfectly
*   and cooperates in your plan for new life*
created in your image.
Help us to support men and women
in their vocation of marriage, especially in difficult times
*   when they join their sufferings to the Cross.*
Help us to uphold the institution of marriage in our
*   society*
as the place where love is nurtured and family life begins.
Help us acknowledge that our future depends on this love
*   and on Your providential care for us. Amen.*

— The Roman Catholic Dioceses of Massachusetts

Nihil Obstat: Rev. Mark O'Connell, J.C.D.

Imprimatur: Sean Cardinal O'Malley, O.F.M. Cap.

Archbishop of Boston

The Sixth Commandment
Part IV: Offenses against the Dignity of Marriage
Section II: Divorce

~

READINGS
Matthew 5:31-32; 19:3-9;
Catechism of the Catholic Church § 2382-2386

The number of divorces in our country is overwhelming, even among those who call themselves Christians. Thus, it becomes necessary to ponder this sad fact, to try to understand this crisis which plagues the institution — the sacrament — of marriage. Divorces are undertaken for countless reasons, some grave and some trivial, but perhaps the primary value that is neglected when divorce is believed to be the only possibility is the value, the power, of forgiveness.

Studies show that those who have decided to divorce and those who have chosen to stay together usually have similar problems. The difference lies not in the difficulties one encounters in marriage, but rather the path that one chooses in an attempt to find a solution to those problems. In the Gospel of St. Matthew, we read:

> And Pharisees came up to him and tested him by asking, "Is it lawful to divorce one's wife for any cause?" He answered, "Have you not read that he who made them from the beginning made them male and female, and said, 'For this reason a man shall leave his father and mother and be joined to his wife, and the two shall become one'? So they are no longer two but one. What therefore God has joined together, let no man put asunder."
>
> — Mt 19:3-6

Here, Jesus quotes from the book of Genesis regarding God's original intent for marriage, a vision that had existed since before the Fall of man, when human life was lived in its most ideal way. We know that our lives are far from such an ideal, yet this fact does not exempt us from striving for, and doing our best to live by, the plan that our heavenly Father has created for us. Even though Jesus admits that Moses granted divorce due to the hardness of man's heart, our Savior still forbids such action, still says that the original plan is possible, livable, preferable. It should be noted that this response of Jesus follows a lengthy discourse on how much one should forgive another, a discourse in which Jesus claims that we should forgive not seven times but seventy times seven times. Perhaps we can think of such extravagant forgiveness as being possible for us only because of the infinite reservoir of grace that our heavenly Father makes available to us. In God we have unlimited forgiveness, unlimited redemption. It has been said that one can do all things through Christ if one only believes. Does "all things" not include saving a marriage?

Marriage is the closest of all possible human relationships. It is the relationship in which we open ourselves completely to another, in which we make ourselves utterly vulnerable. We give ourselves to a spouse body and soul, and in so doing we bestow upon a spouse the power to wound us terribly. We expect to be held lovingly; to be embraced, protected, and accepted unconditionally. When we are not, when we are betrayed instead, we are hurt in ways that defy description. Yet we still must accept Jesus' challenge to forgive as God forgives — fully aware that in every human relationship, forgiveness must be granted over and over again.

Such forgiveness is born in love. It does not expect perfection; it does not set impossible demands. It asks only that the one who is forgiven sincerely try to mend his ways. It is aware that some failure is likely, perhaps even inevitable. It is aware that the person being forgiven is a beloved child of God, a very imperfect person of infinite worth. Such forgiveness is difficult but not impossible. With the help of prayer and the sacraments, by accepting into our lives the forgiveness that Christ won for us, we can become able to forgive in this way, to go beyond the hardness of our bruised and callous hearts and arrive at a place of understanding of forgiveness, a place to begin again, a place in which we can keep whole and holy the Sacrament of Matrimony.

Quotation for Meditation

Finally, I want to recall the sacrament of Matrimony, this "great mystery . . . in reference to Christ and the Church" (Eph 5:32). In marriage, in Christ's name and through him, a covenant is established between two people, a man and a woman, a life-giving community of love. This sacrament is the human participation in that divine love which has been "poured out into our hearts through the Holy Spirit" (Rom 5:5). According to St. Augustine, the third Person of the Blessed Trinity in God is the "consubstantial communion" of the Father and the Son. Through the sacrament of Matrimony, the Spirit forms the human "communion of persons" between a man and a woman.

— Pope John Paul II,
The Spirit, Giver of Life and Love, 354-355

❧ Quiet Time and Then Discussion ❧

Questions for Meditation

1. Discuss why divorce has become so widespread in our culture.

2. Discuss the meaning of forgiveness and how this relates to divorce.

3. What does it mean when Sacred Scripture says "the two shall be one flesh," and what does this mean in terms of divorce?

Prayer

Almighty Father, in Your care for us, You give us the Sacrament of Matrimony to unite a man and a woman in unbreakable bonds of love and faithfulness. Through marriage, You bestow on us the great honor of reflecting in our own lives Christ's infinite love for His Church. Yet we are weak. Far too often, we betray the one to whom we have promised unending devotion, and in doing so we betray You as well. Renew in us, we pray, an understanding of the sacredness of Matrimony. Keep us strong and faithful in our marriages; let us see them as the blessed covenants You have created them to be; enable us to accept joyfully the holiness You graciously offer us in the bonds of matrimony. Amen.

Meditation Twenty-Seven

The Seventh Commandment
Part I: Respect for Persons and Their Goods

READINGS
Deuteronomy 24:14-15; 25:13-16; Amos 8:4-6; James 5:1-6;
Catechism of the Catholic Church § 2407-2418

We are fallen. The biblical story of Adam and Eve announces this sad fact in terms that are difficult to ignore. Willfulness is so basic to our human nature that we regularly choose conflict over concord, even when there is no need. We discover in so many of the tales found in sacred Scripture a portrait of humankind that is highly unflattering — one that shows us to be grasping and self-centered, angry and scheming, duplicitous and vengeful. The biblical authors see in us the one part of creation that has lost its way, that has no idea how to find God, that desperately needs a savior. In their eyes, we are — to use today's parlance — dysfunctional.

And as we look around us, we find this portrait a hard one to deny:

A woman purchases a large order in her local supermarket. Before she leaves the store, she realizes that the clerk has accidentally forgotten to charge her for several items. She pauses a moment, as if torn by indecision, and then walks on, emerging from the store triumphant.

A garage mechanic confronts a troubled customer whose car is making a strange new sound. The customer is sure disaster is on the horizon. The mechanic knows the problem to be nothing serious, although he doesn't bother to share this information. In only a few minutes, he installs an inexpensive new part and then charges his relieved customer for two hours of labor.

A little boy is transfixed by a toy that belongs to his best friend. He is so enthralled he can barely put it down. He begs his mother for one just like it but discovers she thinks it too expensive: he will have to wait for his birthday — months and months away. The boy goes home with the toy tucked carefully beneath his coat.

Such stories don't raise an eyebrow. They are so very understandable, so very human. We excuse them as being mere examples of human nature. And that is exactly what they are: examples of our fallen nature.

In God's Seventh Commandment, we are instructed to resist our fallen nature; we are told that what belongs to others simply doesn't belong to us. Implicit in this commandment is the understanding of property, of ownership; the comprehension that some things are ours, and other things are not. Grudgingly, we are forced to accept this rule as reasonable, and we vow not to steal — although we find ourselves regularly looking for loopholes.

The Seventh Commandment, however, gives us pause in that it almost seems too easy, and much different from the six we have already encountered. Nothing about the Seventh Commandment seems particularly onerous (no matter how often we break it); nothing about it tugs at the soul the way the others do, for in the seventh of God's commandments, we have a law that seems to deal only with *things* — the ones we must not take — not with people or with God.

But our God is a God who has no great interest in things. His interest lies in souls, and so we must look closer to find the real meaning of the Seventh Commandment. When we do, we discover that here, again, God is showing us how to live our lives well and meaningfully in relationship with Him and with others. In the eyes of God, it is not just the object that we steal that makes theft sinful; it is the damage we do to another by taking what is rightfully his — what he may have great need for.

So, while stealing $100 from a millionaire is a clear contradiction of the Seventh Commandment, and an unambiguous sin, stealing the same money from a poor single mother who needs it to buy food for her children is a far deeper descent into sin. It harms her and her children greatly.

Therefore, while our transgressions against the Seventh Commandment may enrich us, they have the potential to do grievous harm to others. Each such transgression shows clearly that we value things over persons — a way of seeing our lives very differently from the way God does. In the Seventh Commandment, God tells us that the desire for things must not be the motivating force of our lives, and that accumulation of objects (of wealth) should not overly concern us; people should. In the Seventh Commandment, we find a direct refutation of what our fallen world considers important; here, we find what God considers valuable. Following the Seventh Commandment, in both large and small matters, makes us and the fallen world we live in a little less dysfunctional and a little closer to God

Quotation for Meditation

Matthew, Mark, and Luke all record the words of the Savior to the rich young man who asked what he should do to gain eternal life. Among other precepts, he was told, "You must not steal."

Immediately, though, Christ added what some have considered the most distinctively evangelical attitude toward worldly possessions. Having told the young man not to steal or defraud, and invited him to "go sell everything you own, and give the money to the poor," and then, "come, follow me," Jesus made a commentary on the man's declining the invitation. "How hard it is," he sadly observed, "for those who have riches to enter the kingdom of God!" The disciples were astonished at this remark, which Christ then repeated, now adding that "It is easier for a camel to pass through the eye of a needle than for a rich man to enter the kingdom of God" (Mk 10:19-27).

Christ does not say that the rich cannot be saved; but he does say that it will not be easy.

— John A. Hardon, S.J.,
The Catholic Catechism, 384

≫ Quiet Time and Then Discussion ≪

THE SEVENTH COMMANDMENT
Part I: Respect for Persons and Their Goods

Questions for Meditation

1. What impels us to steal from others?
2. Is stealing from an institution different from stealing from a person?
3. How does theft, even of small items, damage the people from whom they are taken? How does it damage the one who takes these things?

Prayer

Lord, let me be satisfied with what's mine. Make me content with the life You have given me, the people I know, the possessions that I own. Let me not be grasping and desirous of those things that rightfully belong to others. Give me the grace never to take what is not mine or to long for the passing things of this world. I ask this through Jesus Christ, Our Lord. Amen.

Meditation Twenty-Eight

The Seventh Commandment
Part II: The Social Doctrine of the Church

READINGS
Leviticus 19:9-15; Luke 16:10-13;
Catechism of the Catholic Church § 2419-2436

Our world is full of injustice. Our world is full of inequities. A small number of people possess immense, almost staggering wealth, while a tremendous number of others possess almost nothing at all. Some people live lives of backbreaking labor, yet barely earn enough to feed their children. Others are so rich they could pass their entire lives doing nothing but spending and still die surrounded by opulence. The poorest members of some societies seem unbelievably rich to the average members of others. Starvation and abundance are neighbors; affluence and want coexist uneasily in the same locations.

Holy Mother Church sees all this and declares, in the name of the God who makes every human being in His image and likeness, that such inequality is unnecessary, profoundly wrong, often sinful, and that it is an affront to the Seventh Commandment. Neither "thieves, nor the greedy . . . nor robbers will inherit the kingdom of God" (1 Cor 6:10), writes St. Paul. While most people are neither thieves nor robbers, greed afflicts us all, and those people and nations who amass astonishing excess wealth, while ignoring those who possess nothing, damage not only those they keep in poverty; they damage their own souls, as well.

"Give to him who begs from you, and do not refuse him who would borrow from you" (Mt 5:42), says Jesus during the Sermon on the Mount. A few chapters later, in the same Gospel He adds, "You received without pay, give without pay" (Mt 10:8). In these words from the Bible, we discover the answer to want, the astonishing and unexpected sure cure for world poverty. It is an answer that demands that we act like bearers of the divine image . . . and as if others are, as well. It is so radical a cure that it has never been tried; it is so pure a remedy that it could have come only from God. It is simply that we treat others as real people — that we encounter them as brothers and sisters, share as we would share with a brother or a sister, and love as a Christian is supposed to love.

Our human nature, so tainted by sin, recoils at such a solution. Some people are undeserving; some will take advantage of us; some will use our substance for evil things; they will leave us with nothing. A thousand excuses flood our minds, each one showing how far we are from the people God wants us to be. In truth, such a solution would be unworkable in any society that wasn't populated entirely by saints. But even if we can't bring ourselves to simply hand our hard-earned possessions to those in need, we can still stand with the Church when she tells huge corporations they must pay their workers in Third-World countries more than mere pennies, that underpaying people is stealing from them. We can still work to see that some of the riches of our own highly blessed nation are used to ameliorate the suffering of the poor in nations that have few material blessings. We can still offer our time, talent, and treasure to charities that help those who cannot help themselves, that strive to lessen the inequities between those who have great wealth and those who have nothing. We can still work to moderate our own greed, to make do with less and thus be able to offer others more.

We inhabit a sinful world, and greed is but one of the many sins in which humankind specializes. As greed grasps at every human heart, it is built into every human society. Inequalities are inevitable, and the poor are usually shunted aside and forgotten. As Christians, we must strive constantly to temper the world's greed with justice; we must remind those of great wealth or great power that it is not only a thief or a robber who steals, that those who indulge in the sin of immense greed at the expense of the poor are taking from those who already have next to nothing. Such a heartless thief can have no place in the kingdom of God.

THE SEVENTH COMMANDMENT
Part II: The Social Doctrine of the Church

Quotation for Meditation

Since economic activity is, for the most part, the fruit of the collaboration of many men, it is unjust and inhuman to organize and direct it in such a way that some of the workers are exploited. But it frequently happens, even today, that workers are almost enslaved by the work they do. So-called laws of economics are no excuse for this kind of thing. The entire process of productive work, then, must be accommodated to the needs of the human person and the nature of his life, with special attention to domestic life and of mothers of families in particular, taking sex and age always into account. Workers should have the opportunity to develop their talents and their personalities in the very exercise of their work. While devoting their time and energy to the performance of their work with a due sense of responsibility, they should nevertheless be allowed sufficient rest and leisure to cultivate their family, cultural, social and religious life.

— *Gaudium et Spes*, #67

ᘒ Quiet Time and Then Discussion ᘒ

Questions for Meditation

1. What is the ultimate source of the great inequalities in our world?

2. What must we do as Christians when faced with such inequalities?

3. At what times in my life have I been guilty of the sin of greed?

Prayer

We beg you, Lord, to help and defend us. Deliver the oppressed, pity the insignificant, raise the fallen, show yourself to the needy, heal the sick, bring back those of your people who have gone astray, feed the hungry, lift up the weak, take off the prisoners' chains. May every nation come to know that you alone are God, that Jesus Christ is your Child, that we are your people, the sheep that you pasture.

— St. Clement of Rome,
as cited in *The Oxford Book of Prayer*, 212

Meditation Twenty-Nine

The Eighth Commandment
Part I: Seek the Truth in All Things

❧

READINGS
Proverbs 8:1-9; Daniel 13:1-63; Matthew 5:33-37; John 1:14;
Catechism of the Catholic Church *§ 2464-2470*

We are seekers after truth. We are searchers after meaning. No other of God's creatures wonders and inquires, as we do. No one else asks why things are the way they are and keeps repeating this question for a lifetime. We are thrown into a world of relentless questions, countless riddles, endless densely snarled mysteries. Alone of God's creation we perceive these puzzles, and with this perception comes a disquiet, almost a gnawing at our souls. We must know the truth or we cannot rest. Answers must be discovered or we will know no peace. Riddles must be solved or we will be in torment. We almost envy God's other creatures, who accept creation and live within it peacefully, untroubled by questions, knowing neither future nor past but only now. We try to be like them, but we can't. We continue to yearn for truth, and in this yearning, give birth to science — which enables us to probe the workings of God's universe — and philosophy, daring to suppose that if we think purely enough, we will discover ultimate truth. Our science and our philosophy shower us with thousands of new answers — and millions of new questions.

We are seekers after truth. Our compulsive study of cell and seed teaches us how lives emerge, but the truth of why this should be so, maddeningly, eludes us. From our speck of a planet we stare upwards at the vast expanse of interstellar space; we chart the movements of suns and galaxies; we predict the courses of planets, but the truth of why they exist at all baffles us. We seek after truth in political systems that promise utopia and deliver destruction; in psychology that vows to unravel the secrets of our minds; in mathematics, to which we hope to reduce all things. In all these studies we discover only truths, each one satisfying for an instant before the gnawing begins again, for truth itself remains concealed — a frustrating secret at the core of the plainest things.

We are seekers after truth, but our lives are encumbered by lies. In our dealings with others we deceive and are deceived; we hold secrets too shameful to share and present ourselves to others as people we are not. We meet others partway and, in this partial meeting, are made painfully aware of how far we remain from the ones we care about. Our untruths cause discord and division, and we are pushed farther and farther from what we know to be good. We try to speak the truth as lies tumble from our lips.

We are seekers after ultimate truth, for we sense that all the little truths we discover will end in falsity without it. Science tells us that we are nothing but a haphazard coming together of bits and pieces of matter, no different really from rocks or trees or bacteria. All our history, our great works of art and literature and music, all our acts of compassion, all the love we unaccountably feel for others, all our yearnings tell us that this is nonsense. They send us searching for the truth beyond our many little truths, to the truth that lies hidden *in* all things but is different *from* all things. But all our science and all our thinking fail us in the search for the truth behind truths. This search is doomed, as our efforts to be truthful are doomed, until we abandon our pride and our science and our philosophy, until we stop trying to wrest truth from the physical world and finally admit that truth is not something to be discovered but Someone to be met.

Quotation for Meditation

The inmost spirit lives by truth, by its recognition of what is and what has value. Man expresses this truth in words. The more fully he recognizes it, the better his speech and the richer his words. But truth can be recognized only from silence. The constant talker will never, or at least rarely, grasp truth. Of course even he must experience some truths, otherwise he could not exist. He does notice certain facts, observe certain relations, draw conclusions and make plans. But he does not yet possess genuine truth, which comes into being only when the essence of an object, the significance of a relation, and what is valid and eternal in this world reveal themselves. This requires the spaciousness, freedom and pure receptiveness of that inner "clean-swept room" which silence alone can create. The constant talker knows no such room within himself; hence he cannot know truth. Truth, and consequently the reality of speech, depends on the speaker's ability to speak and to be silent in turn.

— Romano Guardini,
Preparing Yourself for Mass, 14

✎ Quiet Time and Then Discussion ✎

THE EIGHTH COMMANDMENT
Part I: Seek the Truth in All Things

Questions for Meditation

1. What impels the human soul to seek after truth?
2. Can the human mind know ultimate truth?
3. How do the truths we discover during our lives on earth point us to God?

Prayer

~⚬~

Lord, what You say is true. Grant that I may follow Your words in my daily life. Your truth shall teach me, guide me, and protect me. May it deliver me from all evil desires and foolish love. Let me esteem nothing as great, or valuable, or wonderful, except insofar as it makes me better and more pleasing in Your eyes. In this way I shall never be a slave of this earth, but shall walk daily towards Heaven with a holy freedom of heart. Amen.

— Anthony J. Paone, S.J.,
My Daily Bread, 7

Meditation Thirty

The Eighth Commandment
Part II: To Bear Witness to the Truth

READINGS
John 14:6,7;
Catechism of the Catholic Church § 2471-74

As we meditate on the Eighth Commandment, we come to see that it could be considered almost a motto for the Oratory of Divine Love. As Oratorians, we strive to respond to the call of God to bear witness to the truth of God. Of course, all Christians are so called, but we in the Oratory are committed to this in a special way; it is our goal to be witnesses to the truth of God in all aspects of our lives, at every moment in our lives, in a world that shows little interest in the truth. In this challenging work we have wonderful models, such as Pope John Paul II, who bore such witness tirelessly and heroically throughout his life, even when ill health and the frailty of old age afflicted him. Our present Holy Father, Pope Benedict XVI, also lives his life as a beacon of truth. These great and holy men stand in a long line of witnesses to God's truth that stretches back over many centuries, all the way to God's covenant with Abraham. Thus our great legacy of truth consists of the untold witnesses who have preceded our endeavors as Oratorians. We are part of this chain. You may not feel that you or your little group can change much, but you are not alone. There are many on earth and many in heaven supporting you with their prayers. The history of the Church shows us what individuals and small groups can accomplish when they surrender themselves to the will of God.

In his letter to the Romans, St. Paul says, "For I am not ashamed of the gospel: it is the power of God for salvation to every one who has faith, to the Jew first and also to the Greek" (Rom 1:16). We Oratorians must be like St. Paul. We must be without shame as we proclaim and try to live the Gospel during a time when many are antagonistic to it — a time very much like St. Paul's. St. Paul and the other early Christians constituted a tiny and insignificant band, but they planted the seeds from which the Church sprang until it grew all over the world. We, too, need to see our role as that of sowers of seeds, for we bear the same seeds that Paul bore, that Peter bore: the precious seeds of the Gospel, seeds that will one day blossom and bear the fruit of salvation. In our efforts to pray as well as to learn and to live the faith, we are taking the responsibility of bearing these precious seeds of the Gospel, of nurturing them, of helping them to take root in our lives and the lives of others.

Every week, when you open the door of your home to other Oratorians, you are demonstrating that, like St. Paul, you are unashamed of the Gospel. You are saying that Christ Jesus is real and that it is in His name that you gather. We must not forget what the Gospel of St. Matthew tells us: "For where two or three are gathered in my name, there am I in the midst of them" (Mt 18:20). When Oratorians meet, they are not alone, for Jesus is there in all His splendor, wonder, and power.

All Christians are called to deny themselves and take up their crosses. This is yet another way of expressing the call to bear witness to the truth. The Christian life is one of self-sacrifice, something that is difficult and a challenge to us all. At times it can even feel like a type of martyrdom. Such a life can occasionally stretch us to the limits of our faith, but if we remain firm, we will win the prize of all prizes, "the pearl of great price." Whether our lives are easy or difficult and regardless of the type of cross we must carry, the call to bear God's truth is one we must hear and follow at all costs. We will fall short often. Sometimes we will fail miserably. That is simply human, and it really doesn't matter, for we can begin again. We have the Eucharist and the Sacrament of Reconciliation to strengthen us; we have our prayer life to renew us. We rise, we pick up our cross, and always, we begin again.

As we strive to proclaim the truth of the Gospel in our words and especially in our lives, God will bless us in uncountable and unexpected ways. Each of us will know the grace of God as we till the fields of the Lord and plant the life-giving seeds of the Gospel. In the end — or, perhaps it is more correct to say "in the beginning" — we will each hear the famous words from the Gospel of St. Matthew spoken directly to us: "Well done, good and faithful servant; you have been faithful over a little, I will set you over much; enter into the joy of your master" (Mt 25:21).

Quotation for Meditation

Consider, beloved, how the Lord keeps reminding us of the resurrection that is to come, of which he has made the Lord Jesus Christ the first fruits by raising him from the dead. Let us look, beloved, at the resurrection that occurs at its appointed time. Day and night show us a resurrection: the night lies in sleep, day rises again; the day departs, night takes its place. Let us think about the harvest; how does the sowing take place, and in what manner? The sower goes out and casts each seed onto the ground. Dry and bare, they fall into the earth and decay. Then the greatness of the Lord's providence raises them up again from decay, and out of one, many are produced and yield fruit.

In this hope, then, let our hearts be bound fast to him who is faithful in his promises and just in his judgments. He forbade us to tell lies; still less will he himself tell a lie. Nothing is impossible for God except to tell a lie. Then let our faith in him be awakened; let us reflect that everything is close to him.

> — St. Clement,
> from a letter to the Corinthians
> as cited in *The Office of Readings*, 1196

✎ Quiet Time and Then Discussion ✎

Questions for Meditation

1. What part did witnessing for the truth play in the Church's early days?
2. How can you be an effective witness for the truth?
3. Why is it important never to give up in your determination to bear witness to the truth?

Prayer

O Almighty God, let the brightness of your glory shine upon us, so that the Holy Spirit, light of your light, may strengthen the hearts of those who are reborn through your grace. Help us to see our duty clearly and fulfill it courageously for your honor and glory.

— Cardinal Terence Cooke
Prayers for Today, 30

The Eighth Commandment
Part III: Respect for the Truth

⚬⚬⚬

READINGS
Psalm 12; Psalm 43; Sirach 27:16-18;
Catechism of the Catholic Church § 2488-2492

W*hat is truth?* demands Pontius Pilate, shortly before he decrees the death of Jesus. As we read these words in the Gospel of St. John, we can almost hear the disdainful tone in Pilate's voice, the bored certainty that truth does not exist, that it is his to define as he sees fit. Pilate has no need for truth, for he has power. As the representative of Imperial Rome, he holds the power of life and death. Truth, therefore, is whatever he declares it to be. But Pilate is mistaken, and Pilate is blind, for even as he asks his question, the truth in human form stands a few feet away, seemingly powerless, insignificant, apparently little more than a bureaucratic matter to be disposed of efficiently.

How oddly up-to-date Pilate's words sound, and how common they have become. A virtual mantra in our universities, our politics, our media, and even in our religious institutions, the words of Pilate — the denial of truth — form the cornerstone of postmodern thinking.

Experience creates truth, we are told. Each one of us constructs our own truth out of our personal experience. What is true for me is what works for me, what makes sense of my life, what enables me to function. My truth may be very different from your truth; in fact, they may be opposites. But this is no problem, for each remains true... for one person, at least.

Power also creates truth, we are told. Those who control the ever-present media, those who wield political power, have the means to impose their own truth on others. There's nothing really wrong in this because one truth is as good as another, and if a truth, once imposed, is found distasteful, we can eventually abandon it for another.

Consensus creates truth, we are told. What the majority in a society believe to be true is true for that society, and so when most people believed that fetuses were unborn people they were, in fact, unborn people. Now, when many people disbelieve this, they are not. History cannot be trusted, we are told: it is simply a narrative constructed by people looking at things through the prisms of their own truth — therefore, it may have nothing to do with what really happened. Science cannot be trusted: it is but one of many ways to view reality. Language cannot be trusted, because no two people understand the meaning of words in exactly the same way. God cannot be trusted, because God is different for each of us and can never be known directly. Up-to-date religious leaders call religious truth "pluriform" and declare all religions to be equally true paths to the transcendent. Thus, the worship of the Triune God becomes no different from the worship of the willow tree in your backyard, as long as you come away from kneeling before the willow tree with a vague sense of the holy.

Pilate's mocking question has become the world's creed, and so the eighth of God's commandments is rendered meaningless.

But the world, like Pilate, is mistaken. The world, like Pilate, is blind, for the truth still stands before us. The very universe proclaims the existence of truth. A dynamic whole composed of trillions of interlocking parts, all working flawlessly together, the universe shouts at us that it is not mere random matter — that it is, instead, creation, that it is coherent, that its laws hold no matter how insistently we deny them. All life proclaims the existence of truth. Each species is true to itself: bees are not butterflies no matter how hard we claim that they are. Touching one will prove the difference in an instant. Every act of love and selflessness proclaims the existence of truth. No one, no matter what his personal truth, no matter what his values, will see an act of kindness as bad, will find in the infliction of needless pain something good.

As Catholics, we do not see our lives as being composed of meaningless fragments. We laugh at the idea that we can create our own truth, but we are firm in believing that we can perceive truth. We see a thousand concentric circles of truth in our lives, in the lives of others, in the world around us. Each one of them brings us closer to the ultimate truth that stands at the center of all things but which goes as unnoticed today as it did before Pilate. This is the truth for which we must have ultimate respect, the truth that gives meaning to the Eighth Commandment and all the Commandments. This is the truth that is a person: the person who, from the center of all being and the depths of our hearts, proclaims: "I am the way, and the truth, and the life" (Jn 14:6).

Quotation for Meditation

As a remedy for this relativistic mentality, which is becoming ever more common, it is necessary above all to reassert the definitive and complete character of the revelation of Jesus Christ. In fact, it must be *firmly believed* that, in the mystery of Jesus Christ, the Incarnate Son of God, who is "the way, the truth, and the life" (*Jn* 14:6), the full revelation of divine truth is given: "No one knows the Son except the Father, and no one knows the Father except the Son and anyone to whom the Son wishes to reveal him" (*Mt* 11:27); "No one has ever seen God; God the only Son, who is in the bosom of the Father, has revealed him" (*Jn* 1:18); "For in Christ the whole fullness of divinity dwells in bodily form" (*Col* 2:9-10).

— Pope John Paul II,
Dominus Iesus, #5

Quiet Time and Then Discussion

Questions for Meditation

1. In what ways do we deny the truth?
2. How should we respond when told that truth is a matter of perception?
3. How can we proclaim the truth of our faith?

Prayer

O God, keep untruthfulness far from me, and never let me indulge in deceitful speech. Permit me to abhor all lies and rid me of the secret falsities I cherish in the depths of my heart. I yearn for Your truth, Almighty Father. I long for it to shine brightly through my life. Open my heart to Your truth, so that I may make haste to obey Your Commandments. Amen.

The Eighth Commandment
Part IV: The Use of the Media and Arts

⚘

READINGS

Psalms 8; 19:1-6; 33:1-11; 104; 111; Wisdom 7:15-17;
Catechism of the Catholic Church § 2493-2513

As we complete our meditations on the Eighth Commandment, we focus on communication, on the media, and
especially on the arts. The Eighth Commandment, of course,
admonishes us not to bear false witness; it instructs us to be
truthful in all our dealings with others. When we are truthful,
our lives become capable of reflecting — at least faintly — the
absolute integrity of our Creator. Thus, integrity enables us to
better show forth the image of God to others. Maintaining such
integrity is a constant challenge for each of us, and this challenge
becomes enormously magnified when we apply it to the media
and the arts, for these involve communication not between two
individuals but between an individual and large groups of others.

To communicate through today's influential media is to wield great power, which always becomes a dangerous temptation. So, if we wish to communicate with integrity on such a grand scale, perhaps we should follow the model of the first communicator, the original artist. We should look to the Lord in an attempt to discern God's own approach. God communicates to us constantly through His word and through creation; He is the ultimate artist, and all that exists is the "work of His hands." God's artwork does not involve a painting, a concert, a play, or a poem. It involves the universe and all it contains; it involves us. When we meditate on His handiwork, we are left in awe. This is the same kind of awe (although on a far greater scale) that we experience when we contemplate a great work by a master artist.

We have only to look in sacred Scripture to find incident after incident in which the creative splendor of God is at work, where the beauty of God's creation is made manifest. And when we turn from Scripture to the world around us, we are given the opportunity to experience His creation with all of our senses. Inevitably, many of the songs that are sung, the pictures that are painted, and the dramas that are performed are but pale reflections of some aspect of God's creation, mere human imitations of the Lord's incomparable ability to communicate and to create: Every creature — every animal, bird, and insect — is a living poem written by God; a poem that took aeons to finish; one that exists for a moment and then is gone forever, to be replaced by endless others, each unique, each lovely, each breathtaking in its perfection. Fields bursting with new flowers in the spring, the surf pounding against the shore: such have been the subjects of countless paintings. Not one of those paintings could ever capture the beauty infused into their subjects by the original artist. What architect could compare with the creator of the Himalayas, of the Grand Canyon? We look above us at the configuration of countless stars, at the ever-changing moon, and discover a silent, endless symphony; we sense harmony beyond human comprehension; we are left without words.

Made in the image and likeness of God, we, too, create. At their best, pale as they may be, our creations praise the original artist. The first tabernacle carried by the children of Israel in the wilderness was filled with sacred art and vessels for worship. There was no practical reason to carry such things in the desert, but the children of Israel understood that beauty was necessary in the worship of the Lord. In Jerusalem, they painstakingly constructed the Temple over many, many years, sparing nothing to make beautiful the home on earth of their Redeemer. Religious themes have inspired some of the best art in history. Think of the ceiling of the Sistine Chapel; contemplate all the sacred music that has enriched the lives of man and been used in the worship of God.

THE EIGHTH COMMANDMENT
Part IV: The Use of the Media and Arts

The Christian community has been given a legacy of beauty and a mandate to produce and present works of art that are pure and that communicate moral and religious truths to all. To do this, we are obligated to use the latest technological ideas available to us; at the same time, we must exercise the utmost care to be certain that other ideas — many of them beloved of our contemporary culture — never gain footholds in the art we produce. We must create true art and communicate through the media in ways that uphold the message of our Creator and reflect His excellence of workmanship. Such work must never be contaminated by the culture of death in which we live. The art created by the Christian community must reveal God in all His beauty, power, love, and purity. Anything less would be a disservice to Him and a misuse of the gifts He has so graciously given us.

We must take back the arts and the media from the culture of death. In much of contemporary art we find an almost purposeful ugliness; we find a willingness — even an eagerness — to offend and desecrate; we find random elements thrown together rather than order; we find despair rather than hope and childishness rather than grandeur. The media is the same; it has espoused a strongly secular, humanistic, and anti-religious philosophy to several generations, a philosophy that knows no transcendence and has produced disastrous results. As Christians, we must resist such forces and encourage the production of art that is ennobling, that glorifies life and goodness. This is not impossible to do, for we have the original artist — the first communicator — as our model, our helper, and our inspiration; and to Him we sing: "How manifold are Your works, O Lord! In wisdom you have made them all. The heavens declare your glory. The earth reveals Your creative power. You form light and darkness, bring harmony into nature and peace to the human heart."[4]

Quotation for Meditation

The power of expression is not the monopoly of man. Expression and communication are, to some degree, something of which animals are capable. What characterizes man is not only his ability to develop words and symbols, but also his being compelled to draw a distinction between the utterable and the unutterable, to be stunned by that which is but cannot be put into words.

It is the sense of the sublime that we have to regard as the root of man's creative activities in art, thought and noble living. Just as no flora has ever fully displayed the hidden vitality of the earth, so has no work of art ever brought to expression the depth of the unutterable, in the sight of which the souls of saints, poets and philosophers live. The attempt to convey what we see and cannot say is the everlasting theme of mankind's unfinished symphony, a venture in which adequacy is never achieved.

— Abraham Joshua Heschel,
Man Is Not Alone, 4

☙ Quiet Time and Then Discussion ❧

Questions for Meditation

1. How do we see God revealed in the world around us?
2. How have the arts spoken to us on a personal level about God?
3. How can we best use the media to proclaim our faith to a doubting world?

Prayer
An Evening Prayer

Beloved are You, Eternal God,
by whose design the evening falls,
by whose command dimensions open up
and aeons pass away and stars spin in their orbits.
You set the rhythms of day and night;
the alternation of light and darkness
sings Your creating word.
In rising sun and in spreading dusk,
Creator of all, You are made manifest.
Eternal, everlasting God,
may we always be aware of Your dominion.
Beloved are You, Lord, for this hour of nightfall.

— Andre Ungar

Meditation Thirty-Three

The Ninth and Tenth Commandments
Part I: The Problem of Desire

◦◦◦

READINGS
1 John 2:15-17; Galatians 5:16-17; Ephesians 2:1-6;
Catechism of the Catholic Church § 2514-2519

We approach the end of the Decalogue — God's basic commandments to humanity. Already we have learned that we must not kill or steal or deceive. We have been told in no uncertain terms that adultery is forbidden to us and respect for our parents is demanded of us, that we must worship only God, and that we must keep holy both God's special day and His name. Like the children of Israel in the Sinai desert, we find that these demands do not come naturally to us: they chafe; they turn out to be more complex than they seem. Like the children of Israel, we must work constantly to make these Commandments real in our lives — to allow them to transform our relationships, our society. Only two commandments remain. Taking a deep breath, we prepare to encounter them, and when we do, we stop dead in our tracks.

For in the Ninth and Tenth Commandments, we suddenly discover ourselves to be on strangely familiar territory. The Ninth Commandment admonishes us not to covet our neighbor's wife. Is this not the Sixth Commandment reiterated in different terms? The Tenth Commandment tells us not to covet our neighbor's goods. How does this differ from the Seventh Commandment, which warns us that we must never steal? Why do two such demands form the conclusion of the Ten Commandments? Why at its very end does the Decalogue seem to repeat itself, to look backward rather than forward?

Of course, the answer is that it does not. Far from taking us into familiar territory, the Ninth and Tenth Commandments bring us, instead, into an entirely different world. What seem at first glance to be repetitions turn out to be something utterly new. They bring God's demands on us to an even more challenging level, and they present us with problems that the preceding eight commandments do not. The first eight of God's commandments all deal with actions — things we can force ourselves to do, even if we don't want to. In the Ninth and Tenth Commandments, however, we leave the world of actions and enter another world, that of emotions; a world that is not so readily subject to our will; a world in which we are more often controlled than controlling.

"You shall not covet" begin both the Ninth and Tenth Commandments, telling us (according to *Webster's*) that we are not to "wish for enviously," that we are not to "desire inordinately." Whether the object of our desires is our neighbor's spouse or new car, this is a tall order, for intense desires spring unbidden and unwanted into our thoughts; strange and inappropriate yearnings seem to be part of the human condition, an unavoidable aspect of our fallen nature. In telling us that desire which does not lead to action can still lead to sin, the Ninth and Tenth Commandments confront us more personally than do the other eight commandments. In them God's demand enters our souls, our hearts, our very being rather than remaining at our periphery, at the level of our public acts. In the Ninth and Tenth Commandments, we hear God's insistence that we be holy not just visibly but in the privacy of our innermost being. In the commandments that bring the Decalogue to a close we encounter a foreshadowing of the teachings of Jesus, who tells us:

> "You have heard that it was said, 'You shall not commit adultery.' But I say to you that everyone who looks at a woman lustfully has already committed adultery with her in his heart. If your right eye causes you to

sin, pluck it out and throw it away; it is better that you lose one of your members than that your whole body be thrown into hell."

— Mt 5:27-29

Thus, the Ninth and Tenth Commandments demand that we allow ourselves to be divided no longer. They tell us that our thoughts and desires must conform to our actions; that in all we do and all we are, we must conform ourselves to the holy will of God. The Ninth and Tenth Commandments conclude the Decalogue not with a look backward but forward, to a time when through the life, death, and resurrection of Jesus Christ, we are made whole and are finally capable of true holiness.

Quotation for Meditation

Once a man sets his heart on anything immoderately, he loses his peace of mind — the proud man, the avaricious man, how little peace they enjoy! It is the detached, the humble, that live wholly at rest. Strange, how easily a man can be attracted and overcome by some slight, some trumpery affection, if he is not yet utterly dead to self! He has no spiritual fibre; nature (you may say) is still strong in him; he has a bias toward the things of sense. And how should he detach himself altogether from worldly desires? Does he leave them ungratified? It is a constant source of irritation to him. Does anybody thwart them? He is ready to fly into a rage.

— Thomas à Kempis,
The Imitation of Christ, 32, 33

Quiet Time and Then Discussion

Questions for Meditation

1. Have I been guilty of coveting what was not mine? If so, did I fight these feelings or did I permit them to grow?
2. Have I let the things (or persons) that I have coveted become God for me and thus lapsed into the sin of idolatry?
3. Do I appear moderate and in control of my emotions to others while still feeling overpowering yearning for things (or persons) to which I have no right?

Prayer

O Almighty God, eternal Treasure of all good things, thou fillest all things with plenteousness; Thou clothest the lilies of the field, and feedest the young ravens that call upon thee: Thou art all-sufficient in thy self, and all-sufficient to us, let thy Providence be my store-house, thy dispensation of temporal things the limit of my labour, my own necessity the measures of my desire: but never let my desires of this world be greedy, nor my labour immoderate, nor my care vexatious, and distracting, but prudent, moderate, holy, subordinate to thy Will, the measure thou hast appointed for me.

— Jeremy Taylor, *The Golden Grove; or, A Manuall of Daily Prayers and Letanies*, p. 72.

The Ninth and Tenth Commandments
Part II: The Battle for Purity

READINGS
Matthew 5:8; 2 Timothy 2:20-26; 1 Thessalonians 4:1-8;
Catechism of the Catholic Church § 2520-2527

We are of the earth, flesh and blood creatures, and we have much in common with the predators and prey with whom we share our fragile planet, our island in empty space. We are fallen, sinners one and all, each the product of a thousand generations of other sinners. We wonder what a guiltless life might look like but can't quite imagine it. We long for the purity that our sinfulness denies us — but of what does that purity consist? We search for a glimpse of such perfection in the eyes of a small child, but even such a child — years before actual sin can enter his life — has already been touched by original sin; he is already less than God intended. Our substance is dust, the second creation account in the book of Genesis tells us. We can't help but agree. We are of the earth. The purity of heaven is foreign — inconceivable — to us.

But our lives are journeys to God, the One who is ultimate purity. Our lives must be a constant yearning for the purity that we can't quite envision, the purity that was ours before the fall, the unknowable purity of our first parents, the blissful purity of our ultimate destination.

Humankind has striven for purity since its first encounter with God and has constantly fallen short. Our Hebrew ancestors in faith tried to legislate purity, attempting to restore through religious law what we had lost through sin. To this day Orthodox Jews spend their lives painstakingly navigating the corridors of a maze of ritual laws that are designed to produce and preserve purity. Jesus, however, tells us that such an attempt is inadequate. "Not what goes into the mouth defiles a man, but what comes out of the mouth, this defiles a man" (Mt 15:11), He tells us; and then, even more ominously, He says, "Every one who looks at a woman lustfully has already committed adultery with her in his heart" (Mt 5:28). In these statements, Christ links purity with the Ninth and Tenth Commandments, the ones that do not deal with action but with thought and desire. He defines the battleground for purity as our hearts and souls.

"Blessed are the pure in heart, for they shall see God" (Mt 5:8), says Jesus, as He nears the end of the Beatitudes. These words spoken by another could be taken as the condemnation of all mankind, of all earthbound creatures who cannot even understand what real purity is, but Jesus comes to save and not to condemn. In His mouth, these words ring with hope rather than despair. The purity that exceeds human imagination — purity that we can find only in scant traces in our sinful world — is suddenly made real as a gift to all who desire it. The life, death, and Resurrection of our divine Savior create new being, new hope, infinite possibility. From His wounded side flow life, the sacraments, renewal and cleansing, and power that so far exceeds our power that it enters our hearts and souls and wins the battle for purity for us. In Baptism, we are washed clean; in the Eucharist, we are made new; in the Sacrament of Reconciliation, we are freed of our sins. In all the sacraments, we are purified and given the strength to rise above our fallen nature. In the outpouring of God's love that is Jesus, we sinful creatures are made able to be "pure of heart." We are made fit to "see God."

We are of the earth, but in Jesus we discover the astounding truth that we are also of heaven.

Quotation for Meditation

There are two wings that lift a man from the ground, singleness of heart and purity; the one regulates your intentions, the other your affections. The single-hearted man makes for God; the pure-minded man finds and enjoys him. No right course of action will have difficulties for you, if only you're free in your own heart, free from ill-regulated desires. Such freedom will only come to you in full measure when you've made God's will and your neighbour's good your sole aim, your sole consideration.

— Thomas à Kempis,
The Imitation of Christ, 83

Quiet Time and Then Discussion

Questions for Meditation

1. What is your personal conception of purity?
2. Why is it so difficult for us not simply to achieve purity but even to envision real purity?
3. What can we do to bring our relationships and our thoughts closer to real purity?

Prayer

Lord Jesus, You make it very clear in Your teaching that problems in purity are centered in the heart and not simply in external actions and deeds. You promised that the pure of heart will see God. Keep this promise always before my mind, so that I may always seek to do Your will with a pure heart. Amen.

— Fr. Benedict J. Groeschel, C.F.R.

Meditation Thirty-Five

The Ninth and Tenth Commandments
Part III: The Disorder of Covetous Desires

READINGS
Matthew 6:19-21; Micah 2:1-5; 2 Samuel 12:1-6; 1 Kings 21:1-29;
Catechism of the Catholic Church *§ 2534-2540*

We are so ravenously hungry that we could devour the universe. We possess many things, but they are not enough. We need more . . . just a little more . . . perhaps just one thing more. If we get what we want, we'll finally be satisfied, content, at peace. And when that one thing comes, it brings with it bliss — for an instant — and suddenly we're hungry again. Looking enviously at others, we're sure they've never known the hunger that we know, the desire for things to fill our emptiness, to make us whole. Others have so much compared to us; if only we could share a bit in their luck. They don't deserve it any more than we do; in fact, we deserve it more.

218

THE NINTH AND TENTH COMMANDMENTS
Part III: The Disorder of Covetous Desires

Our desires are endless — our wanting, the only infinite thing about us, our envy, an ever-present companion. Against these desires stand two of God's commandments, the ninth and the tenth, reminding us sternly: "You shall not covet your neighbor's wife" and "You shall not covet your neighbor's goods." This, more or less, covers everything we could think of coveting.

These commandments hurt; they tell us that in the eyes of God, our hunger is wrong, that our desire to possess everything is somehow inappropriate. Perhaps God doesn't understand our personal problems, our unique situation. If only He did, He'd comprehend how important it is for us to have just a bit more of what our neighbor possesses . . . and then a bit more, and then still more. We're only trying to fill the emptiness, after all.

But neither things nor other people that we reduce to the status of things can ever fill the emptiness that exists at the center of each soul. Coveting our neighbor's goods or our neighbor's spouse cannot bring us fullness or wholeness but only greater, more intense emptiness. We are not made to own things; we are made to own eternity. Hunger for the goods of this world is a sham. It is a misunderstanding, a mask for our real hunger. We hunger for the Eternal One who made us. We are tormented and empty without Him, so we try to find a substitute — a substitute for the One who can have no substitute. Our misdirected hunger becomes our master; our desire becomes God for us. Our very wanting becomes our idol . . . and so the ninth and tenth of God's commandments bring us full circle back to the first. We are confronted again by the demands of the One who tells us to have no others before Him, who offers us all good things, who feeds us with His Body and Blood, with the food that banishes hunger forever.

Sacred Scripture is replete with examples of people, great and small, who were brought low by their insatiable desire for the things of this world, for the possessions of others, for what was never rightfully theirs. The object desired varies in these stories. At times it is power as in the story of the Tower of Babel; at other times it is sexuality, as in the story of David and Bathsheba. Always, it destroys happiness and leads to more desire, more hunger. In those cases that do not end in total tragedy, the remedy is never found except in turning from the object that was so desired to the One whom we are made to desire.

The Ninth and Tenth Commandments are too difficult for us to manage alone, for they demand that we control the desires of our hearts, and these desires are sometimes far beyond our control. We have but one hope: to turn to the One who is eternity, the One who alone can fill our emptiness. To Him we must say with all our heart, "In Your will is my peace."

THE NINTH AND TENTH COMMANDMENTS
Part III: The Disorder of Covetous Desires

Quotation for Meditation

[As a result of Adam's disobedience] man now has to bear an inner conflict, a conflict quite natural to him. His animal appetites now go after their wants without regard for his better judgment and free will. Even when man wishes to follow his intelligence and strive after better things, he has to fight for control of his unreasoning appetites and blind desires. He no longer has infused knowledge, but must learn the answers to his daily problems by labor and experience.

So often this interior conflict brings confusion to the mind and indecision to the will. Yet man's natural reason is still able to judge good and evil, still able to distinguish truth from falsehood. To save you from all serious doubts, [Christ has given you His] Church to guide your mind and strengthen your will.

— Anthony J. Paone, S.J.
My Daily Bread, 56-57

Quiet Time and Then Discussion

Questions for Meditation

1. What practical things can we do to control our desires?
2. How does excessive covetousness affect our relationships?
3. What are the secret hungers in our lives that keep us far from God?

Prayer

Father, I want too much. I want things to own and people to love me. I want security and abundance, happiness and youth and health, and a thousand other things. I can't stop wanting. Give me the gift of satisfaction, Father. Let me be content with what I have, which is Your endless love. Quiet the yearnings of my heart and permit me to contemplate the truth of the matter: that I am already rich beyond all description. Amen.

The Ninth and Tenth Commandments
Part IV: The Disorder of the Spirit

⚘

READINGS
John 15:12-17;
Catechism of the Catholic Church *§ 2541-2547*

Covetousness is wrong. The Ninth and Tenth Command-ments tell us this unequivocally. Excessive wanting morphs into sin; it leads — subtly and imperceptibly — to estrangement from God. An unusually sly sin, covetousness creeps up on us, pretending to be something it is not — a harmless bit of plea-sure in the use of something, in the presence of someone — and when we have innocently opened the door of our hearts to it just a crack, it boldly enters and refuses to leave. Covetousness feeds on us, devouring us from within like a spiritual cancer, one that grows slowly at first but then faster and faster until it fills us, becoming an obsession. A hidden sin, covetousness tucks itself away inside us as other sins cannot. It permits us to appear healthy — even holy — when, in fact, we have turned far from God.

As Catholics, we understand these things almost too well. We know our hearts to be wayward, our desires endless, and our wills weak. We construct high walls of defense between ourselves and the devourer whom we call covetousness. We know our sexual desires present us with an endless struggle (one easily and frequently lost), so we take pains not to put ourselves in situations in which we will be tempted: we censor our television and movie watching, our reading, our very thoughts; we deny ourselves the company of certain people. We know that our other appetites can be problems as well, so we fast; we purposely do without; we introduce penances into our lives, especially during Lent. They become our spiritual gymnasium, and we become athletes of God. We hope they will confer on us control of desire as an athlete gains control of his body. We strive to achieve mastery over the impulses of the heart, the yearnings of the soul — and we inevitably fail.

We fail, for we insist on doing the impossible. In avoiding the sin of covetousness, we invite the sin of pride to take its place. Long periods of effort, of temptation, failure, and rededication, finally bring us peace; our spiritual athletics seem to pay off. A particular wrongful desire lies vanquished at our feet, and we effortlessly brush aside temptation after temptation. Success is ours; we've just boarded the express train to sainthood. And then, in the midst of our self-congratulations, we surrender without a fight to the very desire we've supposedly eradicated, embracing it, wallowing in it. When we come to our senses, we find ourselves back at square one.

Covetousness cannot be mastered in the way that the other sins enumerated in the Decalogue can. We can erect no walls to protect us from it, for it resides within us. Constantly conflicted, we are a bewildering mixture of saintliness and sinfulness, divided beings, hungering after countless contradictory things. Our desires are intrinsic to our fallen humanity. We cannot transcend them because we cannot transcend ourselves; thus, any victory we achieve over them that depends solely on our own strength will be temporary, provisional. To master covetousness, we must cease to battle it single-handedly. Instead, we must surrender ourselves to the One who transcends all things; we must put aside our pride and stop trying to be athletes of God; we must recall the words of our Savior in His Sermon on the Mount and accept the fact that we will be most blessed when we become poor in spirit, when we admit our powerlessness and ask of the One who is infinite power to heal the conflicts and mend the brokenness of our lives. God's reservoir of graces is infinite — even more infinite than our wants — and God is eager to bring our unruly yearnings under His loving control, eager to transform our covetousness into generosity, our yearning into satisfaction, and our desires of the flesh into the transcendent desires of the spirit.

Quotation for Meditation

Nature is selfish. It will try to enjoy everything on earth and still gain Heaven. Even where sin is involved, nature attempts to make excuses for self and looks for reasons to favor self. Grace simply looks for [Christ's] will, turning away from all occasions of sin and self-deception.

Nature hates all restraint. It wants to follow its own likes, its own desires, and its own will. Grace is interested in self-control, self-conquest, and obedience to authority. It seeks to please [Christ] in everything and in every way. It looks for opportunities to suffer something more for [Christ's] sake.

—Anthony J. Paone, S.J.,
My Daily Bread, 208

⚞ Quiet Time and Then Discussion ⚟

Questions for Meditation

1. Why can covetousness not be mastered in the way that the sins of theft or adultery can?

2. What relationship can the sin of covetousness and the sin of pride have?

3. How can we distinguish a covetous desire from a legitimate desire?

Prayer

Holy Spirit, come to me, free me of my unruly will, my intemperate desires. Give me the grace to love only what is good, only what You command. Permit me to desire only Your love, for if I do, I will find the satisfaction and joy that all the treasures of the world cannot provide. Amen.

On the Third Day He Rose from the Dead

The Resurrection of Christ

READINGS

Matthew 28:1-10; Mark 16:1-8; Luke 24:1-12; John 20:1-9;
Catechism of the Catholic Church § 638-644

There are 52 weeks and 365 days in each year. Each of those days is different, unique. Every one of them is a moment that, once gone, can never be recaptured. But there is one week that stands completely apart from all other weeks of the year, and within it there is a day that is as different from all other days as it is possible to be. I write, of course, of the week that gave birth to the Church, the week that rescues us from death, the week that sets Christianity apart from all other religions and faith systems. And the day I speak of is the day we call Resurrection Sunday, the day that changed the world forever, that day that gives ultimate meaning to human life.

It is mystifying to think that one week has altered time — has altered everything — for over 2,000 years and will continue to do so for eternity. Nothing can reverse what was accomplished on Calvary and at Christ's tomb during the first Holy Week. Throughout His whole earthly life, Jesus of Nazareth was moving toward the events of that week. Even in the despair of the Garden of Gethsemane and the desolation and agony on Calvary, Christ was always on His way to the Resurrection, pointing us to it, preparing to display to the entire world the infinite power of God's love.

The *Catechism of the Catholic Church* says, "The resurrection of Jesus is the crowning truth of our faith in Christ, a faith believed and lived as the central truth by the first Christian community; handed on as fundamental by Tradition; established by the documents of the New Testament; and preached as an essential part of the Paschal mystery along with the Cross" (*CCC* 638).

This miraculous event, this monumental moment, transformed the world and it continues to transform every individual who has truly believed in it. As Christians, we are challenged to face the Cross of Christ — to see beyond it to the Resurrection — and we are challenged to take up our own crosses in imitation of Him. Is our faith in the Resurrection strong enough to enable us to die to ourselves, to trust in the God whose love triumphed in

Christ? Do we dare to believe that this God's love will triumph in our own lives, as well? If we persevere, if we continue to carry our crosses and follow Christ, we will experience the infilling of the Holy Spirit; we will receive newness of life. This is a genuine spiritual rebirth and will enable us to live a new life in the power of the Resurrection.

Each of us undergoes a personal passion as we follow Christ; each of us follows Christ in his own unique way. On the journey to Gethsemane, to Calvary, to the tomb, and to the Resurrection we have the wonderful life-giving opportunity of daily growth, of constant metamorphosis. St. Paul says, "I die daily." In our walk with Jesus we die to ourselves and arise from ourselves while experiencing the new birth. In the Gospel of St. Matthew, Jesus tells us: "And he who does not take his cross and follow me is not worthy of me. He who finds his life will lose it, and he who loses his life for my sake will find it" (Mt 10:38-39).

We, who have faith and believe in Christ, have been saved from eternal death by Calvary and the Resurrection. Through them, the Church has been born, the sacraments have come into being, and God's forgiveness has been made available to us. The sacraments afford us the opportunity to experience ongoing meta-morphosis, a constant deepening of our relationship with God.

The appearance of the risen Savior to Mary Magdalene and the holy women on the day of the Resurrection must have been a life-changing event of the greatest magnitude. Surely, within a matter of seconds, they must have gone from shock and fear to wonder and then to joy unspeakable. As Catholics, we vicariously experience the Passion and death of our Savior every year during Holy Week. Our liturgies can be powerful and emotional occasions that make real to us the terrible and glorious events that took place so long ago. Surely, we can never know those great events in the way that Jesus' disciples experienced them at the time — but just as surely, we can know them in a way that is every bit as profound. We know the result; they did not. We have the Mass, which makes present for us Jesus' death and Resurrection at the same instant; they did not. When the Host and the chalice are raised during the consecration, we should react like the women at the empty tomb, confronted by the risen Lord. "Yes!" we should say. "Our Savior died and rose from the dead and He is alive! Alive! Alive!"

Quotation for Meditation

He was crucified for all, desiring his one death for all to give all of us life in him. It was impossible for him to be conquered by death; nor could he who by his very nature is life be subject to corruption. Yet we know that Christ offered his flesh for the life of the world from his own prayer, "Holy Father, protect them," and from his word, "For their sake I consecrate myself." By saying that he consecrates himself he means that he offers himself to God as a spotless and sweet-smelling sacrifice. According to the law, anything offered upon the altar was consecrated and considered holy. So Christ gave his own body for the life of all, and makes it the channel through which life flows once more into us....

When the life-giving Word of God dwelt in human flesh, he changed it into that good thing which is distinctively his, namely life; and by being wholly united to the flesh in a way beyond our comprehension, he gave it the life-giving power which he has by his very nature. Therefore, the body of Christ gives life to those who receive it. Its presence in mortal men expels death and drives away corruption because it contains within itself in his entirety the Word who totally abolishes corruption.

— St. Cyril of Alexandria,
"Commentary on the Gospel of John," as cited in
Christian Prayer, The Liturgy of the Hours, 1991

✌ Quiet Time and Then Discussion ✌

Questions for Meditation

1. Discuss how Christianity is different from the other religions of the world.
2. How did the Resurrection of Jesus transform humanity?
3. Think carefully about how Christ has transformed your own life. Try to imagine what your life would be like if you did not know Christ.

Prayer

O Lord Jesus Christ, Your Resurrection is the very foundation of our faith. Your crucifixion and death only have meaning insofar as You are victorious over death and the forces of Hell. As we face the challenges, difficulties, and sufferings of life, help us to always keep before our minds Your glorious Resurrection; help us to be able to be witnesses to that Resurrection and to eternal life to those whom we meet along the way. We pray through Christ, Our Lord. Amen.

— Fr. Benedict J. Groeschel, C.F.R.

Notes

1. Will Herberg, *Four Existentialist Theologians* (New York: Doubleday, 1958), 9.

2. Francis S. Collins, *The Language of God* (New York: Free Press, 2006), 102.

3. Paul Tillich, *Systematic Theology, Vol. I* (Chicago: The University of Chicago Press, 1951), 211.

4. *Gates of Prayer* (New York: CCAR, 1975), 335.

Works Cited

Unless otherwise noted, all quotations from sacred Scripture are taken from the *Revised Standard Version, Catholic Edition*. In addition to such quotations and those from the *Catechism of the Catholic Church*, the following works were either cited or used in the preparation of the meditations in this volume.

St. Clement, "A Letter to the Corinthians," *The Office of Readings* (Boston: The Daughters of Saint Paul, 1983).

Francis S. Collins, *The Language of God* (New York: Free Press, 2006).

Cardinal Terence Cooke, *Prayers for Today* (Staten Island, NY: Alba House, 1991).

Cyril of Alexandria, "Commentary on the Gospel of John," in *Christian Prayer, The Liturgy of the Hours* (Totowa, NJ: Catholic Book Publishing Corp., 1975).

Walter Farrell, O.P., S.T.M., and Martin J. Healy, S.T.D., *My Way of Life* (Brooklyn, NY: The Confraternity of the Precious Blood, 1952).

Four Existentialist Theologians, ed. Will Herberg (New York: Doubleday, 1958).

St. Francis de Sales, *An Introduction to the Devout Life* (Rockford, IL: Tan Books and Publishers, 1994).

Gates of Prayer, ed. Chaim Stern (New York: CCAR, 1975).

St. Gregory of Nyssa
—"Homily on Ecclesiastes" in *The Liturgy of the Hours* (Totowa, NJ: Catholic Book Publishing Corp., 1975).

— "Christian Perfection" in *The Office of Readings* (Boston: The Daughters of Saint Paul, 1983).

Benedict J. Groeschel, C.F.R.

— *The Courage to Be Chaste* (Boston: Paulist Press, 1985).

— *The Virtue Driven Life* (Huntington, IN: Our Sunday Visitor, 2006).

— *Heaven in Our Hands* (Ann Arbor, MI: Servant Books, 1994).

Romano Guardini, *Preparing Yourself for Mass* (Manchester, NH: Sophia Institute Press, 1997).

John A. Hardon, S.J., *The Catholic Catechism* (New York: Doubleday, 1981).

Abraham Joshua Heschel

— *Man Is Not Alone* (New York: The Noonday Press, 1951).

— *The Sabbath* (New York: The Noonday Press, 1951).

Thomas à Kempis, *The Imitation of Christ* (Fort Collins, CO: Ignatius Press, 2005).

C. S. Lewis, *Mere Christianity* (New York: Touchstone, 1996).

St. Irenaeus, "Against Heresies" in *The Office of Readings* (Boston: The Daughters of Saint Paul, 1983).

Pope John Paul II, *The Spirit, Giver of Life and Love* (Boston: Pauline Books and Media, 1993).

Christopher P. Klofft, S.T.D., *Living the Love Story* (Staten Island, NY: Alba House, 2008).

Peter Kreeft, *Making Choices* (Ann Arbor, MI: Servant Books, 1990).

Blessed Columba Marmion, *Christ, the Life of the Soul* (Colorado Springs, CO: Zaccheus Press, 2005).

John Henry Newman, *Prayers, Verses and Devotions* (Fort Collins, CO: Ignatius Press, 1989).

The Oxford Book of Prayer, ed. George Appleton (New York: Oxford University Press, 1985).

Anthony J. Paone, S.J., *My Daily Bread* (Brooklyn, NY: The Confraternity of the Precious Blood, 1954).

Karl Rahner, *Prayers for a Lifetime* (Chestnut Ridge, NY: Crossroads, 1995).

Cardinal Joseph Ratzinger (Pope Benedict XVI), *Introduction to Christianity* (Fort Collins, CO: Ignatius Press, 1990).

Siddur Sim Shalom, ed. Jules Harlow (New York: The Rabbinical Assembly, 1985).

Jeremy Taylor, *The Golden Grove; or, A Manuall of Daily Prayers and Letanies* (R. Royston at the Angel in Ivie-lane, 1655).

Paul Tillich, *Systematic Theology*, Volume I (Chicago: University of Chicago Press, 1951).

Vatican Council II, The Conciliar and Post Conciliar Documents, ed. Austin Flannery O.P. (Collegeville, MN: The Liturgical Press, 1975).

The Vatican II Sunday Missal (Boston: The Daughters of Saint Paul, 1974).

* * *

Papal documents not cited above have been taken from the Vatican Web site, www.vatican.va.

All quotations from the documents of the Second Vatican Council have been taken from *Vatican Council II, The Conciliar and Post Conciliar Documents*, which is cited above.

The English translation of the Non-Biblical Readings by Cyril of Alexandria, St. Clement, and St. Gregory of Nyssa is from the

WORKS CITED

Liturgy of the Hours © 1974, International Committee on English in the Liturgy, Inc. (ICEL): excerpt from the English translation of the Preface for Marriage III from the *Roman Missal* © 1973, ICEL. All rights reserved.

The prayer that appears on page 206 by Andre Ungar is taken from *Siddur Sim Shalom,* © 1985. Used by permission of the Rabbinical Assembly.

Use of quotations from *My Way of Life* by Walter Farrell, O.P., S.T.M., and Martin J. Healy, S.T.D., as well as those from *My Daily Bread* by Anthony J. Paone, S.J., is graciously granted by the Confraternity of the Precious Blood, 530 Fort Hamilton Parkway, Brooklyn, NY 11219; www.confraternitypb.org.